CW00382912

The Homecoming

The Homecoming

Kay Bagon

Copyright © 2017 Kay Bagon

The moral right of the author has been asserted.

Apart from any fair dealing for the purposes of research or private study,
or criticism or review, as permitted under the Copyright, Designs and Patents
Act 1988, this publication may only be reproduced, stored or transmitted, in
any form or by any means, with the prior permission in writing of the
publishers, or in the case of reprographic reproduction in accordance with
the terms of licences issued by the Copyright Licensing Agency. Enquiries
concerning reproduction outside those terms should be sent to the publishers.

Matador
9 Priory Business Park,
Wistow Road, Kibworth Beauchamp,
Leicestershire. LE8 0RX
Tel: 0116 279 2299
Email: books@troubador.co.uk
Web: www.troubador.co.uk/matador
Twitter: @matadorbooks

ISBN 978 1788039 796

British Library Cataloguing in Publication Data.
A catalogue record for this book is available from the British Library.

Printed and bound in Great Britain by 4edge Limited
Typeset in 11pt Minion Pro by Troubador Publishing Ltd, Leicester, UK

Matador is an imprint of Troubador Publishing Ltd

For Paul, Robin and Keren

CHAPTER 1

By the time Katy was finally allowed to go home it was almost dark and the street lights were sputtering into a reddish glow. Her heavy schoolbag cut sharply into her shoulder as she walked slowly along the road, reflecting on the devastating news she had just been given.

The day had started badly; to be accused of cheating in an *art* exam must surely rate as the most ridiculous of charges. True, she had written down a few dates of birth of some well-known painters on her shirt cuff, but none of them had featured in the test anyway. And how unfair of Miss Simms to send her to the Deputy Head for such a minor offence.

Katy had found herself joining the band of troublemakers, queuing up outside the office door which bore the dreaded words, 'Deputy Head'. Mrs Field, the incumbent, was not noted for her patience, rarely allowing anyone the chance to even begin to offer an explanation for their misdemeanours; indeed her icy stare could reduce a child to such a state of terror that they became unable to utter a single word in their defence. But Katy, stung by the seeming injustice of the accusation that she had been a cheat, and having a determined nature, had unwisely attempted to argue her case.

'This is the third occasion that I have had to see you this week, Katy. What is it this time?' snapped Mrs Field.

'Well, Mrs Field,' said Katy innocently, 'it's just that Miss Simms thought that I was cheating in the art test.'

Mrs Field looked at her coldly. 'And were you?'

'No, *of course* not,' said Katy emphatically. She tried to keep outwardly calm, although she was burning with defiant anger.

Mrs Field's eyes narrowed. 'Then why did Miss Simms think you were cheating?' she persisted, coldly.

'Well, I had written down two dates on my sleeve,' Katy explained, 'but I didn't look at them because the questions weren't actually…'

Mrs Field glared at her.

Katy noticed with interest that her face was gradually developing bright red blotches.

'That's quite enough,' Mrs Field declared. 'You were obviously intending to cheat. This school will simply not tolerate cheats and liars. You can go straight into lunchtime detention, where you will write an essay on the evils of dishonesty and a letter of apology to Miss Simms.'

Katy stared at her. Mrs Field's face was now very red indeed.

'But I *did not* cheat,' she objected.

'Don't you argue with *me*, child!' thundered Mrs Field. 'And you can go *now*!' she shouted, as Katy continued to glare at her rebelliously.

Katy left the office angrily, pulled a face and gave

the thumbs down sign to the rest of the queue waiting anxiously outside. She walked deliberately slowly down the main staircase, and reluctantly joined the group of children in the detention room. Katy sat down at the back and gazed out of the window. If only she could join her friends in the playground…

She was soon lost in her own thoughts, but was sharply brought back to earth by the rasping voice of Mr Frapp, the teacher in charge of the detention room.

'Well, Kathleen Warner, so you're here once again. Can't say I'm surprised. Have you not been set any work? I'm sure I can find you something to do.'

Katy glowered at him. She hated being called by her real name. No other teacher did that.

'I actually have an essay to write,' she replied at length, deliberately missing out the word 'sir'.

'I have an essay to write, *sir*,' said Mr Frapp, predictably. 'Well then, I suggest you get on with it, Kathleen.'

Katy sighed very loudly, picked up her pen, then after some thought wrote a very short letter of apology to Miss Simms; but couldn't help adding that in fact she had *not* actually cheated. She signed it, 'Yours very faithfully, Miss Katy Warner'.

Eventually she started to write a rambling composition about how cheating was a way to try and gain an unfair advantage over others, and that you were also not being honest with yourself; but even though she wrote in very large handwriting she found that she had only managed to cover half the page. What else could she say? In fact, she could think of several reasons why telling lies might sometimes be a *good* idea, such as not hurting someone,

3

or to avoiding getting somebody else into trouble. There was still fifteen minutes of detention time left. Why not include them too? Surely, for a balanced essay, she ought to take account of both sides of the argument.

Mr Frapp had been using the time to catch up with marking some French homework. As the hour was nearly up, he wandered round the desks collecting up the extra work that the children had been set. Most of these consisted of pages of lines and various written corrections to previously marked work. Since Katy's was the only essay, he idly read it to while away the remaining few minutes of the detention. Then he frowned, pushed his chair back, and called Katy out to his desk.

'Kathleen, what *is* this? You were told to write an essay about why cheating in an exam is *wrong*. You do not appear to have done so. I'm sorry, but I shall have to show this to Mrs Field. Now go and sit down!'

Katy stood her ground. 'But I've written a good essay. I only wrote what I thought was—' she began indignantly.

Mr Frapp stood up and banged the desk crossly with a ruler. He was obviously keen to go to lunch himself now, and in no mood to argue. 'Right,' he said to the rest of the class, 'with the exception of Kathleen Warner, you can all go.'

He turned to Katy. 'Kathleen, I am now setting you a further detention tomorrow lunchtime, as you evidently need more time to reflect on the error of your ways.'

'But that's so unfair!' shouted Katy, her eyes brimming with tears at the injustice of it all. She grabbed her school bag and stormed out of the room after the others, banging the door loudly behind her. She could hear Mr Frapp shouting at her to come back at once, but she ran on down the corridor, ignoring his cries, and out into the playground where she sat under a tree and moodily ate her sandwiches.

Why should she be given another detention? For what? It was absolutely ridiculous. Well, she wouldn't turn up!

Lunch break was nearly over. Katy was utterly fed up. She just wanted some peace and quiet. But her two best friends had spotted her sitting there and came running over, shouting, 'Hi, Katy, where've you been? We've been searching for you all over.'

'I've been stuck in lunchtime detention,' replied Katy crossly. 'I've only just got out,' she added, between mouthfuls of apple.

Then she suddenly remembered the Plan. Gosh, it was meant to happen today. Oh no, she really wasn't in the mood at all. Maybe they could postpone it…

Carole looked at her thoughtfully. 'But today's the big day, Katy. You haven't forgotten have you?'

'We *are* going ahead with the Plan, aren't we?' added Jane. 'I mean, you're not chickening out or anything, are you?'

Put like that, Katy instantly denied that any such thought had ever entered her head.

After all, it was true, they had planned it very carefully; Jane had stolen an official sheet of headed school notepaper from the office. Carole had taken the sheet home and carefully typed out:

WEDNESDAY 14th NOVEMBER 1962
AT 3.30pm THE SCHOOL WILL BE HOLDING A

FIRE PRACTICE.

WHEN THE FIRE ALARM RINGS EACH FORM IS TO
ASSEMBLE IN THE SCHOOL PLAYGROUND.

A.R. KNIGHT
Headmaster

It had been decided that Katy's task was to find an unsuspecting First Year child who wouldn't ask any questions, and instruct him to take the note round to every classroom. Then, at three-thirty exactly, she'd ring the fire alarm. Piece of cake!

It would be great; they'd interrupt their boring double Chemistry practical session that afternoon and provide an entertaining diversion. Also, Katy kept reminding herself, it would really serve a quite useful purpose, as the school had not held a fire practice since last year.

Just then, the school bell went. Katy stood up, solemnly took the sheet of paper from Carole and placed it carefully in her satchel.

'Of course you can rely on me. The deed will be done,' she assured them, as they strolled back into school together. 'See you in the playground at half past three.'

Katy could never resist a challenge!

CHAPTER 2

Katy was one of the first to arrive in the Biology laboratory. She was surprised to see that Dr Butler was already there, busily drawing a large diagram of a heart in coloured chalk on the blackboard. No wonder she always found herself trying to catch up in his lessons; not that she had actually attended very many this term.

As usual, Dr Butler was wearing a pin-stripe suit, waistcoat and, his speciality: a polka-dot bow tie, of which he seemed to have an unlimited supply. He was Head of Science, and was always very formal, as if to remind everyone of this significant fact. Katy was sure that he regarded himself as more a university lecturer than a school teacher.

Dr Butler and Katy were sworn enemies. He managed to find fault in everything that Katy did, and on the slightest pretext would exclaim, 'Katy Warner, you are yet again causing a distraction to those around you. Kindly remove yourself to the back of the laboratory.'

Katy would then find herself sitting far away from her friends at the wooden bench at the back of the laboratory, facing away from the blackboard. The bench was completely empty apart from a fish tank where a sad-looking axolotl resided, perched on a rock, half in and half out of the water. As a result of her frequent enforced moves, Katy had much opportunity to study him. He was a strange prehistoric-looking white creature, with four little legs, pink gills and black staring eyes. He only ever seemed to get excited when he was fed by the technician, who gave him pieces of raw liver which he would suddenly pounce on and devour in one go.

The motor of the pump, which kept the air bubbling through the water in his tank, had a very annoying whine. As soon as the noise in the laboratory rose, Katy would turn off the tank regulator, to see how long it would be before the resulting silence became apparent, then she would quickly switch it back on again. Her record to date was only ten minutes, after which Dr Butler would shout, 'Katy, why have you turned that fish tank off again? How many more times do I have to tell you? The water will turn green and cloudy. Turn it on immediately and go and stand outside the door if you can't behave!'

And inevitably, Katy would be sent out of the laboratory, where Dr Butler would conveniently appear to forget her. Indeed, much of Katy's school day would be spent standing outside various classroom doors, keeping an ear and an eye out for the Headmaster's approach, when she would casually walk straight past him, pretending merely to be on her way to the toilet, or on a mission. In fact, it was surprising that Dr Knight never seemed to think it at all odd that he was constantly passing her in the corridor.

Today, however, Katy was so preoccupied with the impending fire practice that she sat quietly through the whole lesson. She was suddenly brought back down to earth by the sound of Dr Butler's voice.

'Katy, are you not feeling very well today?'

'I'm absolutely fine, thank you, sir.' But as he continued to stare at her doubtfully, she added more reassuringly, 'Just a bit tired, that's all.'

She was only too aware that she was anxiously glancing at the clock every few minutes, and when the bell finally went for the next double Chemistry lesson she leapt up and was first out of the Biology laboratory. She raced down the stairs as fast as she could. It was five to three and there were only a few minutes during the lesson change-over to find someone to take the precious fire practice announcement, which Carole had so carefully typed out, round to every classroom in the school.

Who could she ask? She felt very conspicuous, hovering anxiously in the corridor. She must find someone soon. Just then a small First Year boy approached. He'd do.

Katy leapt out in front of him and said, in what she thought was a commanding voice, 'Excuse me. There is to be a fire practice this afternoon and the Headmaster, Mr Knight, has instructed me to find a reliable messenger to take this letter round every classroom in the school.'

The small boy gazed up at Katy with surprise. He seemed to be unsure of what he was being asked to do.

'You must take this letter to every classroom, *now*. Around the whole school,' Katy repeated more urgently.

The boy seemed quite pleased to have been chosen for such an important mission, and took the letter from her more readily, asking, 'Shall I go *right* now or wait for the bell?'

But before Katy could reply, the bell went, and as she was herself very keen to leave, she replied rather sharply, 'Just go!' And, as the little boy hurried away down the corridor, clutching the letter in his hand she shouted after him, 'Thank you!'

Katy ran back up the stairs and into the Chemistry laboratory. Soon the rest of her set joined her.

Chemistry was taught by an elderly teacher named Dr Fry, but called 'the Prof' by just about everyone in the school – including the staff themselves – behind his back. He was noted for his unfailing ability to ensure that none of his practical demonstrations ever had the expected result. For this reason, his lessons were hugely popular. He always carried out his experiments on the front bench, and everyone would crowd round to watch, enthusiastically offering unhelpful advice or making witty observations, all of which he either did not hear or just chose to ignore.

'Right, Class 5B,' the Prof announced, 'I'm going to show you how to do a simple titration of acid against alkali, then you can work in pairs and repeat titration yourselves. Everyone, please come to the front bench.'

They didn't need a second bidding. The whole class surged forward, jostling for the best view. Katy managed to squeeze into the front row.

'Safety glasses, everyone! They're in the box on the side bench. Sit further back from the apparatus, please.'

No one moved. 'Right, please pay attention,' Dr Fry slowly continued. 'In this flask we have some dilute hydrochloric acid. I shall gradually be adding some dilute sodium hydroxide, which is an alkali, from the burette. At the endpoint, you will see the colourless solution in the flask turn pink . This is called the point of neutralisation. I have calculated that this should take about 20 millilitres of alkali. We have already covered the theory behind it. Does everybody understand?'

'Yes, yes, we know all about it. Can we get on with the demo, sir,' they chorused.

Everyone sat round on their stools expectantly, and for a short while there was actually silence as they watched the Prof gradually add more and more alkali to the flask, until the burette was completely empty. The liquid in the flask, however, remained as clear and colourless as a glass of water.

A chorus began. 'Gosh, that was truly amazing, sir!' 'How do you know it's pink, sir?' 'Your best demo yet, sir.' 'It's not working is it, sir?' 'Boring!' 'Pour some more acid in, sir.' 'Shall I check your calculations for you?' The comments echoed around the laboratory. The noise level rose.

As usual, the Prof looked completely baffled. He feebly raised his right hand towards the students and said ineffectively, 'Will you all stop calling out please. There is evidently a slight problem. I'll have to go and fetch the technician from the prep room.'

Dr Fry left the lab amid cries of, 'She'll sort you out, sir.' And then, 'Sir, I can smell gas! There's a gas leak, sir!'

He soon returned with Barbara, the chemistry technician, in tow. The class cheered.

Immediately, the technician noticed the unopened bottle of colour indicator still sitting on the bench. She picked it up, waved it at the Prof, and said rather loudly, as if addressing an infant, 'Oh look, Dr Fry, you've forgotten to add the indicator. No wonder it hasn't worked. Just try adding a few drops to the flask.'

Katy smiled, half expecting Barbara to pat the Prof gently on the head.

Sheepishly, Dr Fry followed the technician's advice and the solution in the flask immediately turned a bright pink colour.

A huge cheer rang out across the laboratory: 'Yeeeeeees!', and some of the pupils began to stamp their feet and clap.

Attempting to regain some sort of control, Dr Fry banged the wooden board rubber on the bench and shouted, '*Quiet* please! I will carry out this experiment again if you just sit *silently*, otherwise you will all have to return to your benches and write up the experiment by yourselves. And please,' he added more forcibly, 'turn those gas taps off, *now!*'

The Prof stood for some time and glared at the class, waiting for them to be quiet. Eventually his threat had the desired effect and the class sat more quietly and watched transfixed as the technician set the experiment up again. Meanwhile. Dr Fry patiently tried to explain why the demonstrate had failed.

'We missed the point of neutralization,' he droned on, 'only because the phenolphthalein indicator was not present. I shall therefore just repeat the titration, using the indicator, and you will see for yourselves that it will work. Just bear with me, please.'

But no one was listening to his explanation. Everyone

was impatient for the fun to begin again. Someone began to sing, 'Why are we waiting? Why are we waiting? Why are we waiting? Why, oh why.'

'OK, Dr Fry, it's all set up,' said the technician finally.

Once again the class crowded round the bench, transfixed. The noisy comments began again, 'Shall I stir the flask for you, sir?' 'Don't forget the indicator, sir!' '*Why* are you doing it again, sir?' 'Good luck, sir!'

Ignoring the interruptions, the Prof bravely added a few drops of the indicator solution to the flask and once again started the titration. However, much to his surprise, he had added only two drops of alkali from the burette when the solution in the flask immediately turned bright pink again.

Howls of laughter and more ribald remarks greeted this result. 'It doesn't work, does it, sir?' 'You said it needed 20 ml, sir.' 'Shall I try again for you?' 'It's rubbish, sir. Shall I get the technician again?'

The Prof stepped back from the bench and gazed at the pink liquid, shaking his head in disbelief. He looked more perplexed and uncertain than ever, and examined each of the bottles of chemicals in turn. Finally, he took his safety glasses off put them on the bench and rubbed his nose thoughtfully. He looked at his watch and then up at the clock.

Deciding to abandon the whole experiment, he said rather weakly, 'I'm sorry, but there isn't enough time to try this again, so just return to your benches. *Quietly*, please.'

The fun was over. The class reluctantly returned to their benches, having thoroughly enjoyed the demo, and Dr Fry decided for the umpteenth time that he really must try out his demonstrations beforehand. (It never seemed to cross his mind that the chemistry technician, who had a brother at the school, might be deliberately causing many of his problems.)

Still laughing at his disquiet, Katy looked up at the clock again. Gosh, it was already twenty-six minutes past three. That little First Year boy must have gone round most of the school by now, and was in all probability heading back towards the Science Block.

She had to go. Asking to go to the toilet, she left the Chemistry practical abruptly, and ran swiftly up the stairs to the third floor of the Science Block. She'd made sure that the Physics Laboratory would be empty… but where on earth was the fire bell? She should have checked beforehand.

Katy stood still for a minute. She began to panic as the enormity of her crime suddenly hit her. Where *was* the bell? She could feel the sweat running down her face.

There it was, next to the window. Oh, no! She'd have to actually break the glass front of the fire bell! She hadn't realised that. What could she use? The minutes were ticking away… Maybe her shoe? But her hand shook so violently against the button that she knew she had completely lost her nerve. She dare not break the glass!

Katy stood there transfixed for a minute, breathing rapidly. Should she just abandon the whole idea? But they'd all think she'd just chickened out. This was awful! What about ringing the school bell? Surely no one would notice the difference. It was that or nothing! She pressed and held on to the button of the school bell for as long as she dared.

The sound was absolutely deafening, since she was standing directly beneath the bell itself. Louder still was the sound of her own heart thumping like a pneumatic drill through her body.

Katy had absolutely no idea how many minutes passed as she held on to the bell. The noise reverberated unbearably through her head. She fought hard against the strong inclination to let go and run down the stairs. What if someone should come upstairs to search the Physics Laboratory for missing students? Any minute now, someone would see her standing there. She couldn't hold on to the bell much longer.

Gradually Katy became aware of the sound of people rushing along the bottom corridor and, from the upstairs window, saw that groups of children were beginning to file out into the playground. Judging by the noises coming from one floor below, everyone was leaving the other laboratories too. She had better go.

Finally letting go of the bell, Katy dashed down the stairs to find that the corridor was absolutely packed with excited children all jostling their way out of the Science Block.

She allowed herself to be swept along by the crowd and out of the door, arriving in the playground, where a scene of complete pandemonium greeted her. Teachers were frantically trying to get their forms to line up so that they could be checked off on the register, but no one seemed to know where to go.

Dr Fry had forgotten to bring his register and was trying to check his form by asking who was missing, and who was actually absent, while still wearing his lab coat

15

and, unaccountably, clutching a bottle of acid in his hand.

Mr Knight, the Headmaster, was completely distraught, since he was unaware that this was in fact a practice and assumed that there was actually a fire. He ran across the playground, shouting, 'Has anyone called the fire brigade? Have all the classrooms been checked? Where *are* all my staff?'

As nonchalantly as she could, Katy joined her own class and got her name ticked off on her form register. This was relatively easy, as no one had even noticed her absence. She slowly began to relax and survey the confusion and consternation that was taking place amongst the school staff and the Headmaster. She spotted Carole and Jane in their class line. They smiled and gave her the thumbs up sign. This was really excellent. Their Plan seemed to be working better than they could ever have imagined.

It was the PE teacher who finally managed to restore some sort of order by blowing his whistle loudly and shouting repeatedly at everyone to line up.

Mr Knight called a hasty huddled staff meeting, and eventually announced, 'I have to inform you all that, thankfully, there is no fire. Accordingly, I expect you to file quickly and calmly back to your individual classrooms forthwith. Each form is to proceed in year order, starting with Year One. There will be absolutely no further disruption. You will proceed normally with your lessons.'

By then it was nearly four o'clock and, thinking that the matter would end there, Katy gradually settled back down to her Chemistry practical. It was therefore a terrible shock when about twenty minutes later she saw Mr Knight, the Headmaster, enter the Chemistry laboratory accompanied

16

by the same, very frightened-looking, small boy to whom she had given the original letter.

Everyone stood up in silence. Mr Knight had a very stern manner but, because his sentences were usually so full of long and mystifying words and phrases, few children were able fully to understand him. Katy even kept a notebook full of his particularly unusual statements. (Her best phrase to date was, 'it is invidious to particularise'!).

Mr Knight strode into the middle of the room. 'Excuse me, Dr Fry,' he trumpeted, 'my little friend here is seeking to identify the girl who had the temerity to instigate an unauthorised fire practice in school this afternoon. To this end, we are visiting every room in the building. We shall leave no stone unturned. Such egregious behaviour is construed by the school authorities to be entirely inappropriate and as such, totally unacceptable!'

There was total silence. No one moved. Katy felt very sick. She swallowed hard and looked down at the bench.

To the small boy at his side Dr Knight added, more gently, 'Can you recognise the girl, Phillip?'

Katy had been working on the back bench of the laboratory, and as she was still wearing her chemistry safety goggles fervently hoped that if she kept her head down there was a chance that Phillip might not recognise her. She could almost feel the silence in the room now. Despite herself, she knew that her face was gradually reddening. She wanted to sink into the ground, but the rest of the class seemed to be equally uncomfortable and ill at ease. Even the Prof was gazing guiltily at the floor, and looked as if he himself must in some way be to blame.

Through the silence came an uncertain little voice. 'I think it's that girl there, sir.'

Phillip obviously felt very unhappy. All his self-esteem seemed to have evaporated and he looked as though he was sure that this must be entirely his fault.

Katy remained doggedly staring down at the gas taps on the bench. She was acutely aware that everyone had turned round to see where the child was pointing. After an eternity, she forced herself to look up. Her heart missed a beat as she saw that the small boy was nervously pointing his inky finger at her.

'Katy Warner, eh?' exploded Mr Knight. 'Well, I can't say that I'm entirely surprised. So, Katy, what have you to say?'

Class 5B held its breath, but for once Katy could think of nothing at all to say.

'Right then, Katy, you will take off your safety goggles and accompany me to my office immediately. Thank you, Dr Fry,' said Mr Knight grimly.

Katy felt that her legs were made of lead. A great buzz spread throughout the laboratory. She forced her reluctant feet forward, and unwillingly followed the Headmaster and his scout out of the room.

She soon found herself joining two other possible culprits whom Phillip had also, but wrongly, identified. The three of them were instructed to line up against the wall.

'Gosh, where's the firing squad?' thought Katy grimly.

'Now then, Phillip,' said Mr Knight in a more kindly manner, 'can you be sure which girl it was who gave you the letter? Take your time if you aren't certain.'

This time, however, the little boy had become a good deal more confident, and was unerringly able to identify Katy.

'It was her, sir. I know it was. She gave me the letter!' he cried eagerly.

'Thank you, Phillip,' said the headmaster slowly, 'you have been very helpful. Now please do go back and rejoin your class.' And he opened the door of his study to allow Phillip to walk triumphantly out.

To the other two girls he added, 'Thank you for assisting me in this important matter. I must apologise for any aspersions that might have been cast upon your good characters. You are free to go.' Then, more roughly, 'Katy Warner, wait here.'

Mr Knight went out of his office to summon the Deputy Head, Mrs Field. A few moments later they returned.

'Stand there please, Katy.' And Katy stood facing them across his desk. There was a short silence. 'I'm sure you realize that this is a matter of paramount importance, Katy,' began Mr Knight, 'and that the ramifications could be very serious indeed.'

He stared at her over his glasses. 'What have you to say for yourself?'

At first Katy categorically denied all knowledge of the episode, but lying wasn't her strong point, and after prolonged and intense questioning from the two of them she was finally forced to confess.

'I am deeply disappointed in you, Katy. You have not only let the school down by your behaviour, but you have also let down your parents and yourself. You have been immeasurably irresponsible…'

But Katy had stopped listening. His words were merging into a distorted sound blur. She stared miserably down at the blue carpet beneath her feet. Gradually his voice rose, compelling her to listen.

'… and today you have deliberately attempted to undermine *my* authority. That note was a blatant forgery. Forgery is a *criminal offence*. Through your thoughtless actions you have placed your position at this school in jeopardy. I am going to discuss this with my Deputy. Go and wait outside my office.'

The going home bell sounded and suddenly the corridor was full of children, rushing passed her and running down the stairs. Several children congratulated her – 'Brilliant fire drill, Katy' – and her classmates shouted, 'Good luck!' It was all very well for them, but what about her? She was the one standing outside Dr Knight's office, while they were all cheerfully going home for tea.

Presently the school became silent again. An age seemed to pass as she waited there. What a disaster this had been. What did he mean by, 'placed your position at this school in jeopardy'?

Finally, Mr Knight came out and called her into his office. 'Right, Katy. Mrs Field and I are unanimous in our decision. We have absolutely no choice but to expel you forthwith. You are a disruptive presence within this school and exert an insidious influence on other pupils. I will telephone your parents directly, to arrange for an immediate meeting. Go and collect your things, and return to this office.'

Katy was completely stunned. A sudden hollow sensation filled her stomach. She fought back the tears.

She wouldn't give him the satisfaction of seeing her cry. Expelled! She had never, ever thought that the consequences of the Plan could be so devastating.

She stared at him for several moments in disbelief, then, saying nothing, walked as haughtily as she could out of his office and ran downstairs to the cloakroom. She flung open the toilet door and locked herself in. Now the tears were unstoppable. She must cry silently. Impossible. Her shoulders shook as she sobbed. Thank goodness they'd all gone home. No one must see her like this. She had to calm down.

Katy cautiously opened the toilet door. Good. No one was around. She stared at herself in the washroom mirrors. Her face was all blotchy, her eyes bloodshot. What a mess she looked! She blew her nose on an unforgivingly rigid paper towel and splashed cold water on her face.

She noticed that she was still catching her breath in sharp intakes. Katy sat down on the bench in the changing room. They must be wondering where she'd gone. She ought to collect her satchel and her coat. Well, they'd just have to wait!

Walking at a snail's pace back along the corridor and up the main staircase, she eventually arrived at the Headmaster's office. Well, at least this would very probably be the last time she would ever be summoned here. She took a deep breath and knocked uncertainly on the door.

'Come in, Katy. I have to inform you that, regrettably, I have been unable to obtain a reply to my telephone call to your home, and that consequently I am instructing you to hand this letter personally to your parents. It contains a request that they telephone my office first thing in the morning. Your parents must confirm that they will attend a meeting with me tomorrow, to facilitate your immediate removal from the school roll. Now, I am ordering you to leave the school premises, forthwith!'

Thus it was that Katy was now the unwilling bearer of the worst letter imaginable. How on earth was she going to tell her parents that she'd been expelled? And how would she be able to sit her O-level exams?

Katy was still completely wrapped up in her own thoughts when she arrived some fifteen minutes later at her house, opened the gate, and walked up the garden path.

CHAPTER 3

The house was in complete darkness. After a prolonged assault on the front door knocker, Katy was forced to acknowledge the fact that Mr Knight had been right: no one was in. It began to rain.

Where was the door key? Katy searched her pockets. She found her purse, an old bus ticket and a screwed-up paper towel. It must be in her satchel. It had to be. But after a careful search she had to admit to herself that, yet again, she had forgotten to take it with her. What a pain, and she was getting really soaked. There was no alternative; she'd have to go round to the back of the house and climb in through the upstairs bedroom window. This unconventional means of entry was by now almost routine, as Katy invariably seemed to find herself locked out.

She threw her school bag off her shoulder and went to retrieve a stout garden cane which she had hidden behind the shed. Then she began to climb up the precarious drainpipe, which was barely attached to the wall by rusting brackets, holding the stick with her left hand. The manoeuvre was more difficult than usual, since the rain had made the drainpipe very slippery, and Katy found herself rapidly sliding all the way down again.

She gritted her teeth; if she didn't get in soon, she'd be wet through. She forced herself to try again, and at the third attempt finally succeeded in reaching the top. Now for the risky bit; leaning across, she carefully inserted the stick though the upper small half-window, which was always left open (her mother being a strong proponent of 'fresh air'), and managed to dislodge the lower window catch. Edging slowly along the window ledge, she pulled the lower window open, using her fingernails. Dropping the stick back into the garden she carefully climbed into her father's bedroom. Closing the window again, she stood still for a moment to catch her breath.

There was complete silence. Katy wondered if there might be an intruder hiding somewhere in the house. She stood and listened for a tell-tale creak but all she could hear was the sound of her own heart racing from her exertions in gaining entry. She shivered and turned the light on. Sitting down on the bed to get her breath back, she surveyed the rarely used bedroom.

A heavy walnut wardrobe stood alongside the solitary bed. Its door was permanently ajar as it leant awkwardly against a matching four-drawer tallboy. Along the top of the tallboy were photographs of her father's parents.

She could barely remember her grandparents, since they had died when she was only six. If she thought very hard she could conjure up a picture of her grandma. She remembered her as a very small, frail old lady who spoke only in Yiddish, but who always gave Katy a box of mint creams whenever she went with her father to visit her.

Katy relaxed and allowed her thoughts to wander. The best part of their occasional visits to her grandparents' Highbury flat had been meeting her three little cousins there. In fact, the real highlight of each visit was the novelty of racing her cousins down to the bottom of the garden, and peering over the top of the high brick wall, to watch the trains go rushing by below. Although why that should be such an abiding memory was a mystery.

Many more photographs adorned the mantelpiece above the huge grate, which contained an old gas fire. Katy found herself gazing up at a sepia photograph of her father's distant relatives. A family of six stared unsmilingly back at her. Seated stiffly on either side of the front row were the mother, wearing a long black dress, and the father, in a black suit and sporting a cravat. Between them sat two girls, and three boys stood behind, the tallest in the middle. Katy stared at the little girl in the front row. She had a huge black bow in her hair and wore a white dress with a sailor's collar, black boots and long white socks. Katy often wondered how old the girl was, and what she was called. She knew that the family had lived in Poland and owned a jewellery shop. But in 1941, during the war, because they were Jewish, they had all been taken away to Germany and had never been heard of again. Katy's father wouldn't tell her any more than that. She'd asked him many times why they had all been killed, but he would only tell her that almost every Jewish family in Poland had suffered the same fate.

Looking at all the photos, Katy though it strange that there were no pictures of either herself or her mother. The past was evidently of greater importance to her father than his present family.

How cold and unwelcoming her father's bedroom was. The only indication that it had ever been lived in was the presence of her father's old dark blue dressing gown, hanging forlornly behind the bedroom door. The sight of it made Katy feel very uncomfortable. It was almost as if she had somehow trespassed into her father's secretive world.

She glanced up at the clock, but it had long ago given up the struggle of marking the inexorable march of time. Suddenly she remembered that she had left all her things outside in the rain. She jumped up, and carefully stepping over the untidy piles of unread scientific journals and unanswered letters which lay by the side of her father's bed, she opened the bedroom door and peered cautiously along the empty landing. It was a relief to close the door behind her, and her mood lightened a little as she dashed down the wooden staircase with its familiar and comforting creaks on the third and fourth stairs, and went into the kitchen.

Unlocking the back door, Katy rushed out into the driving rain and retrieved her sodden school bag from the top of the coal bunker where it had been unceremoniously abandoned. Dropping the wet bag on the kitchen floor, she took off her damp blazer and hung it on the back of the chair. Gosh, it was already quarter to seven. No wonder she was so hungry.

The kitchen table fitted snugly into a recess in the kitchen wall. Katy reached up and pulled it down, to reveal a cutlery drawer and small cupboard containing jam, sugar and condiments, hidden behind it. Then pulling out the matching wooden seat from the wall along side, she sat down.

Immediately her thoughts returned to her disastrous day. Why had *she* been the one to send the note round the school? And why had she volunteered to ring the fire bell herself? She couldn't believe how naive they'd all been to imagine that they'd get away with it. No one had actually thought the idea through. There were three of them in on it, so why couldn't Jane or Carole have rung the bell? But she knew the answer: she'd been only too keen to gain the admiration of all her friends by executing such a daring scheme. How stupid it all seemed now. Her thoughts kept returning to the jubilant little boy, pointing accusingly at her. The dreadful feeling of that moment would be very hard to forget.

Katy sat for some time staring into space. She sighed deeply. How could such a ludicrous scheme have ended like this? It was so monstrously unfair. Her despondent thoughts soon gave way to pangs of hunger. She must find something to eat.

Rummaging through the larder she discovered the remains of a rather old fruit loaf. She could almost hear her mother's voice saying, 'Katy, you can't possible eat that, dear. It's so stale. Put it out for the birds.' But her rumbling stomach soon overcame any doubts she had concerning its freshness and she cut the loaf into thick slices, spreading it liberally with butter and jam. Pouring herself a glass of milk, she ate the food standing up and then grabbed a handful of chocolate biscuits as she passed the biscuit tin on her way out of the kitchen into the gloomy hall.

The solid oak front door allowed very little light to filter through its tiny frosted window. The old horseshoe hanging below the window served only to produce an additional clatter when the door was opened or closed. It certainly failed to bring any sort of luck or happiness into this cheerless household.

The dark yellow walls of the hall were adorned with several dreary paintings, bordered by a wooden pelmet which held a collection of assorted china vases and pots. The largest painting depicted a dull Dutch interior, with four people sitting round a table in a room with a black and white chequered floor, on which was a crumpled piece of paper. (Katy always wondered why no one had bothered to pick the paper up.) The origin of the painting was unknown and Katy suspected that the previous owners of the house had probably abandoned it when they moved out. Her parents seemed completely oblivious to the general murkiness of the house, and Katy could not recall any attempts at modernisation ever to have taken place.

She walked across the hall, and her footsteps on the creaking floorboards briefly broke the silence. The stillness, although a little frightening, was at least preferable to the sound of her parents' voices raised in unremitting argument with each other, or the noise of doors being aggressively slammed; events which occurred regularly whenever her mother and father were both at home, before each retired angrily to their separate rooms.

She could still hear their angry voices in her head: 'You knew full well that your lunch would be ready by one thirty! Where on earth have you been, it's gone two o'clock?'

'Well I'm here *now*. Stop making such a blasted fuss about it. All you had to do was produce a piece of boiled chicken. It's not as though you are asked to prepare very much!'

'You sit in that damn library every Saturday on your way home from synagogue, just reading the papers, and you know that the soup is boiling dry!'

'Oh, I haven't got time for all this every weekend. I'd like my lunch, if it isn't too much to ask.' And her father would storm into the dining room and shut the door with a bang.

To which her mother would retort, 'Katy, come here, please. Just give your father his dinner from the oven, and tell him that it's *all dried up!*' And the kitchen door would be slammed shut too. Stalemate!

Since her father only used the dining room, while her mother's sanctuary was the lounge, they rarely encroached on each other's territory; but Katy had to act as the go-between. It was like living in two separate houses under one roof, which was just about bearable unless her parents were forced to communicate with each other, inevitably resulting in a bitter argument.

Katy peered into the lounge. Maybe her mother had left some clue as to where she had gone.

The huge chestnut tree growing in the front garden cut the light from the front rooms of the house, both upstairs and down. Its long branches almost enveloped the house on one side, and reached out into the road on the other, scratching the tops of passing buses. The roots of the tree were doing their utmost to undermine the foundations of the house, and several cracks had appeared in the walls, which were beginning to show signs of subsidence, but Katy's mother professed such a great affection for the tree that she would not allow it even to be trimmed.

Katy switched on the light. How old-fashioned the room looked; it was almost like stepping onto the stage setting of an Edwardian play. The walls were decorated with heavy gold brocade wallpaper, which her mother had insisted upon against everyone's advice, and semi-drawn plum-coloured velvet curtains hung from the pelmet to the floor. A worn Indian carpet, which retained its original colours in only a few areas, covered the floor.

A huge red-brick fireplace dominated the room, but it was seldom used since the neighbourhood had recently been designated as a smoke-free zone. Nevertheless, an elegant set of coal tongs and pokers hung in hopeful expectation that one day they might play a crucial role in counteracting the icy atmosphere.

Yes, it certainly looked as though her mother had recently been in here. There was a half-completed *Telegraph* crossword on the coffee table by the burgundy chaise longue, and two cigarette ends in the ashtray. She noticed the open door of her mother's record cabinet (in which Wagner vied for space with Donizetti, while Joan Sutherland was pressed up tightly against Tito Gobbi), and several sleeves from her mother's voluminous collection of gramophone records were lying on the floor. She could just imagine her mother sitting there, propped up by cushions, in the semi-darkness, listening to Grand Opera on the gramophone.

The bookcase next to it was also half open. It was filled with a range of classics, poetry and plays lovingly collected over the years. Katy idly picked up the book which was lying half open on the floor. Glancing at the cover she noticed that it was *Bleak House*. How very apt.

Replacing the book, she wandered over to the window. She could remember when they had first moved in to the house. Aged three, she had struggled to peer over the windowsill to see the front garden. Life had been so much simpler then…

She swung round abruptly, collecting her thoughts. Well, since her mother had most probably gone into town, there was nothing more to be gained in here.

As she passed the mahogany piano, she couldn't resist lifting the lid. What a mixed blessing this gift had been! When she was five she'd been so delighted with such an amazing present, but now, more often than not it was the cause of many arguments and battles.

Her mother loved playing the piano and was really keen for them to play duets together, but Katy hated practising. Scales and arpeggios were so pointless and tedious; besides which, there were always so many other more important things which needed to be done whenever her mother suggested she played. Normally she would only practice the day before a lesson, but now, as no one was here to listen to her, she sat down on the piano stool and began to play the Mozart sonata that she was learning.

She was just starting to lose herself in the music and banish the tormenting thoughts from her head when the telephone rang. At last, someone to talk to. She shut the piano lid, jumped up and ran to answer the phone.

CHAPTER 4

'Hello, it's me,' said a well-known voice. Then, as Katy said nothing, the voice added, 'It's me, Carole.'

'Sorry,' said Katy, 'I was just—'

But she had no time finish the sentence, as Carole continued excitedly, 'It was really brilliant, wasn't it? The Plan worked so well. We were in the middle of a horrendous Latin test when the bell went and by the time we got back it was too late to finish it. But wasn't it weird how quickly the bell stopped? Someone must have turned it off. Maybe it was Mr Knight. He was going absolutely berserk in the playground, rushing round like a mad man. It was so funny; did you see him?'

'Yes, I did,' replied Katy, and was very tempted to tell Carole just how angry he'd been about it. But she stopped herself and merely agreed, somewhat half-heartedly, 'Yeah, I suppose it did go to plan, but did you hear what happened afterwards?'

'Well, I heard some rumours that you got called to see Mr Knight. So how did they find out, then? Everyone's dying to know what actually happened.'

'Oh, well, that brainless First Year told them it was me that gave him the note,' explained Katy in an unconcerned voice, determined to play it down. There followed a short silence. Katy found herself meticulously studying the black Bakelite telephone with its round dial.

'So, do they know about the Plan then?' Carole asked, more anxiously. 'I mean, you didn't mention that Jane and I were…' she faltered.

'*Of course* I didn't say that anyone else was involved,' replied Katy sharply. 'Surely you know me better than that!'

'We were pretty certain that you wouldn't have said anything,' said Carole, rather too quickly. 'It's just that Jane and I wondered if you were OK. There were so many different stories flying around. Everyone was talking about it. You're really famous now, you know!' There was another long silence. 'So… what do you think will happen now?' she ventured at last.

'Oh, I expect that my parents will be called in again,' replied Katy lightly.

She was determined not to mention the impending expulsion, word of which would have spread around the school like wildfire, even if only her 'trusted' friends knew about it. And she certainly didn't want Jane's sympathy now. Nor did she want to admit how upset she was, or how she was dreading telling her parents.

'You sure you're OK? You sound a bit down.'

'No, I'm fine. Look, I've really got to go now,' she lied, 'I'm right in the middle of supper. See you tomorrow and I'll tell you all about it then. Bye, Carole.'

'Bye!'

Katy put the receiver down, wondering why she hadn't been able to be more honest with her friend. Oh well, they would all find out soon enough.

She stood for a long time in front of the antique china cabinet, looking intently at an oriental china coffee set and decanter with little cups made of deep red gilded glass, bought by her father on one of his many trips abroad. The only sound in the room was the small, almost apologetic tick of the clock on the mantelpiece.

Katy's thoughts ran away with her again. If only she hadn't agreed to their ridiculous Plan. Admittedly, it had actually been her own idea, but they should have stopped her. Why did she have to take the blame? Mr Knight hadn't even asked her whether anyone else had been involved, so sure was he that she was responsible. Now they'd all be returning to school tomorrow as if nothing had happened, while her life was ruined. Completely ruined! It was so unfair.

She walked dejectedly out of the room and forced herself to try and think of what she should do right now. Maybe a drink would raise her spirits. Her father always helped himself to a gin and tonic the minute he walked though the front door.

The drinks cabinet was kept in what was known to her family as the 'dining room', although she could never recollect her mother ever to have actually eaten a meal in there. It probably should have been called, 'Father's sitting room', she thought absent-mindedly, since her father used it exclusively when he was at home during the weekends. Katy wondered for the hundredth time why it was that her father's work meant that he lived in Birmingham from

Monday to Friday. But then her mother seemed only too happy with the arrangement.

In contrast to the lounge, the room overlooked the back garden and was often bathed in sunlight, the faded yellowing carpet illustrating the fact. An oval mirror with a green glass surround reflected even more light into the room.

As she opened the dining room door, the clock on top of the sideboard chimed cheeringly. It had such a beautiful square walnut face and resolutely sounded out each quarter of an hour with a peal of bells, as if determined to maintain some sort of order in this fragmented household.

The drinks cabinet was actually a large Art Deco chestnut sideboard, with two cupboards on either side, in which her father kept a large and varied supply of drinks, brought back from his many business trips abroad. Over the years, Katy had furtively investigated the contents of all the variously shaped bottles. Luckily, her father never seemed to notice the drop in the level of the spirits, and it certainly never occurred to him that any one other than himself might be savouring the occasional tipple. Fetching a glass from the kitchen, Katy searched the cupboard for something suitable.

What should she try this time? She poured out a little vermouth. It was quite bitter; you'd have to be really desperate to drink that. She decided to choose a drink she knew she liked, and helped herself to a very generous measure of cherry brandy. Hopefully this would put her into a more cheerful frame of mind. She drank it rapidly and immediately felt its warming effect as it went down. A drop more? Maybe later.

It would have been nice to sit down now and watch TV, as all her friends no doubt were. If only her father had managed to install a television set… but the mere mention of his intention had caused such uproar and dissent that the very foundations of the family had been sorely tested.

'Katy,' her father had called out to her as he arrived home one Friday evening. 'Katy, where are you? I've got a special surprise for you. It's in the car, but you'll have to help me to carry it in.'

Katy rushed downstairs excitedly. Such events were very rare in this household.

'What is it, Daddy?'

'You'll never guess… I've finally bought a television, Katy! I'm going to put it in the dining room. Come and have a look.'

'*What* are going to do?' demanded Katy's mother, appearing suddenly from the lounge. 'You have not consulted *me* about this, Richard. You know very well that *I do not ever* want a television in the house!'

'It's alright, I'm going to put it in the dining room, *you* won't have to see it,' said her father evenly. 'Be reasonable, we're in 1962; it's not the Dark Ages. Everyone has a TV set now.'

'You are certainly *not* putting it in the dining room, or anywhere else. If that television enters this house then *I* shall be leaving it!' declared her mother and she returned to the lounge, closing the door conclusively behind her. The raucous strains of Wagner's *Valkerie* abruptly filled the house.

Katy and her father stood in the hall, staring at each other in silence. They were well aware that Katy's mother had always considered television viewing to be an unnecessary distraction.

'Sorry, Katy,' said her father. 'I thought that if it was actually here she might relent…' He tailed off lamely.

Nothing further was mentioned on the subject, and her father had yet to put his wife's declaration to the test. In fact, it was only after days of argument and begging that Katy had finally been permitted to resume her visits round the corner to the house of Mrs Weeten (who was the grandmother of her best friend, Madeleine), to watch a weekly episode of *Z Cars* on their black and white television. And this, of course, was always the very first privilege to be lost should Katy misbehave.

Indeed, the existence of *that* television set was only deemed to be a justifiable necessity because Mrs Weeten's husband, Madeleine's grandfather, was a semi-invalid and was confined to the house. (Katy had been told that he was mugged whilst taking a bag of diamonds to the bank in Hatton Garden, where he had worked as a diamond merchant. The first Madeleine's grandma had heard of the matter was when several newspaper reporters had knocked at her door, hoping for the full story!)

Oh well, she'd get soaking wet if she went over to the Weetens' now, and besides, they weren't even expecting her. Katy put the glass down and drew the curtains. Music, that's what she needed to cheer herself up!

The radiogram stood on a small wooden writing desk, the contents of which always remained a fiercely guarded secret. This bureau belonged to Katy's mother, and therefore by rights shouldn't have been in here at all, but then there was just no room for it in the lounge.

Katy experimentally tried to open the lid, but as usual it remained firmly locked. She tuned the radiogram to 208, Radio Luxemburg. It was quite reassuring to hear the cheerful voice of the announcer.

Helping herself to another cherry brandy, Katy sat down in the armchair and switched on the table lamp. It was really so cold in the room, but the only source of heat was a small 'Otto' coal stove. It was very old fashioned, with a horizontal sliding door with small windows of black mica. To light it you had to use a gas poker, but it was such a palaver that Katy couldn't be bothered.

Many of her father's documents seemed to have spilled over from his upstairs office, and lay around in disarray on either side of the fireplace. There were piles of old letters, books and magazines, all evidently connected to the mysterious world of Metal Finishing – the field in which her father was a consultant. And that, mused Katy, was the real problem: Metal Finishing occupied her father's life to the exclusion of almost everything and everyone else.

Sipping the drink, she pensively studied the long bookshelf next to her. You could actually imagine what a person might be like, just by looking at their book collection. Her father's consisted of a collection of twenty-four burgundy-coloured volumes comprising the entire *Encyclopaedia Britannica*, 1956, arranged in alphabetical order. They were quite useful, though, for researching topics set for homework. Next to them stood two editions of the Old Testament (in Hebrew and English), three copies of the *Authorised Daily Prayer Book* and a set of black leather-bound Jewish textbooks, with gold-printed Hebrew titles.

It was certainly true that religion played a large part in her father's life. You could always hear him diligently saying his prayers in his bedroom every morning before coming downstairs for breakfast. How many times had she knocked on his bedroom door or called him to the phone during this ritual, knowing full well that he'd always ignore her and just recite his prayers even more loudly?

Her father went to synagogue every Saturday morning and was also a member of a synagogue in Birmingham. Unfortunately, this religious fervour was not reciprocated at all by her mother, who only attended the local synagogue on the Jewish New Year and the Day of Atonement (when it was absolutely unavoidable), even then only staying for part of the service. That was just another matter on which her parents couldn't agree.

Katy put the glass down and took out the *Hagadah*, the Passover prayer book. She turned to the front page, which read:

Parents' Association Prize.
Awarded to
Katy Warner
for
Sabbath Attendance,
5717 1957

She smiled to herself. That was a joke; it should have been awarded to her father, since it merely reflected the fact that he had insisted that she went to synagogue with him every Saturday morning.

When she'd been very little it hadn't been too bad, sitting next to her father in synagogue, but she could still remember when the synagogue warden had told her that she was too big to sit downstairs with her father and she'd have to go upstairs and sit in the ladies' gallery. She had been so upset. She didn't know any of the women up there, all in their elegant hats and stylish clothes. She'd felt so out of place. None of her friends were there. Finally her father had relented, but it was only recently that she'd at long last been allowed to play in school netball and hockey matches on a Saturday morning. Why was everything such a struggle in this family?

Her father seemed permanently wrapped up in his past. How many times had she heard the story about how her father's parents had arrived in England as penniless immigrants, fleeing the pogroms in Russia? Her father had been a tiny baby in his mother's arms. Travelling by night with a small group of refugees, they had been smuggled over the border into Poland by a border guard. Apparently, the Russian guard warned his mother that if her baby cried out, it would put the lives of the whole group in danger, and he would have to smother the child! Luckily the baby slept on, blissfully unaware of his possible fate, and the family eventually reached England.

Katy knew that the family had settled in the East End of London and that they had lived in a small flat over a Jewish bakery shop, where Katy's grandfather worked. Over the years, four more children were born, and money was in extremely short supply, but as her father was always keen to remind her, by studying hard he finally won a scholarship from the local secondary school to read

Chemistry at Imperial College London, and managed to help support his family.

Since both of Katy's grandparents had now died, his brothers and sisters generally regarded her father as the head of the family, as he was the eldest. Because none of her aunts or uncles had gone to university, they were very proud of their brother for gaining a doctorate, and they held his work in the field of metallurgical consultancy in high esteem. They were forever telling Katy that she should show her father more respect. But what was it to do with them, though? Surely being a professional expert didn't necessarily mean that you were a good parent. What did they know?

Surprisingly, her father employed both his sisters and Katy's older cousin as secretaries at the Institute of Metallurgy, where he himself worked. But in order to avoid any allegations of favouritism, he never revealed to the other members of staff that the secretaries were in any way related to him. They had worked there now for many years, and whenever Katy phoned the Institute of Metallurgy she always had to be careful not to ask to speak to 'Auntie Leah', but to enquire if 'Mrs Rubens' was available.

Katy's mother was certain that after all this time the other, non-family, secretary must have suspected something, if she hadn't known the truth all along. But no questions were ever asked, and when the office cleaner suddenly gave in his notice Katy's father was able to employ his own brother Stanley to fill the role. So it was indeed a family affair.

Katy had no doubt that her father was an expert in his field. He had published several definitive textbooks on the subject of metal corrosion and plating, and he often went jet-setting around the world sorting out various technological and manufacturing problems.

She looked up at the framed OBE, which had pride of place above the fireplace. It was signed, in large script, 'Elizabeth R'. Her thoughts went back to the day that her father had received it. She could recall being so enthralled at the idea of actually meeting the Queen that she'd even allowed her mother to choose a smart blue suit for her without objecting, and had actually worn it without protest. The whole day was totally brilliant. The three of them travelled to Buckingham Palace by taxi, and her father wore a top hat and tails. They celebrated with a superb lunch in a first-rate hotel in London.

Yes, her father must be exceptionally clever, Katy considered. None of her friend's parents had such an honour, and they'd been amazed when she told them about meeting the Queen. She knew that her father had been awarded the OBE in recognition of some ground-breaking work that he had carried out in protecting the casing of British fighter-bombers during the Second World War, but she wasn't sure exactly what he had done. It would be good to ask him to tell her about it sometime.

She sighed. Yes, the day of the OBE they had been a really happy family; so why had things gone so badly wrong? The trouble was, her father was so immersed in his work that Katy always felt he had no time for her at all. Thinking about it, when was the last time that she'd ever had the chance to discuss anything really important with him? Never.

Almost unbelievably, her mother claimed that even she didn't know the address in Birmingham where her father lived during the week. But then, her mother had never shown the slightest interest in finding out. Her father simply drove away on Monday morning, returning in time for the synagogue service on Friday evening, when her mother would light the Shabbat candles.

Katy could see that her mother was much happier when her father was not at home, and in fact she and her mother seemed to get on much better then too. Katy sometimes wished that he'd stay away indefinitely.

She'd been lucky, though; his week-long absences meant that her father was completely unaware of her ongoing battles with the school authorities, or of the subsequent suspensions that frequently followed. Basically, neither of her parents had much idea what was going on, so this was going to come as a real shock. She sighed again and put the book back. How on earth was she going to break it to them?

Despite the soothing drink, her worries began to return. No, she wouldn't let herself get all worked up again. She *must* try to focus on something else. It might be an idea to go and read in her bedroom; at least there was a heater in there. She turned the music off, and closed the drinks cabinet. Then, after carefully washing up her glass, she slowly climbed the creaking stairs. It was going to be an awfully long night!

CHAPTER 5

Shutting the bedroom door, Katy sat down on the bed and gradually unwound. The room was quite small, but it felt very secure. Surrounded by her own familiar possessions, she began to feel more comfortable.

It was an escape, a haven, away from the battlefield that encompassed the rest of the house, and at times she almost preferred her own company to being with friends. Even her parents knew better than to walk in unannounced.

She picked up her guitar and began idly to strum a few chords. Should she put the record player on and play along with the harmony? No. She couldn't be bothered; somehow today she just wasn't in the mood.

Katy was quite proud of the fact that she'd taught herself to play the guitar; copying the fingering of the chords from the guitar book. As a rule, time would just zip by as she listened for hours at a stretch to the record player or recorded the latest hits from the radio onto the tape recorder. If she turned the volume up, any sounds of discord coming from the rest of the house could be effectively drowned out. Usually she would be so completely absorbed in the music that it was only when there was a frantic banging on the door, accompanied by the sound of her mother shouting, 'Katy! Katy, I've been calling you for ages. Your supper's ready. For goodness sake, dear, turn that awful noise down!' that she would ever emerge.

'Blowin' In The Wind' was one of her all-time favourites. The chords were quite difficult to remember and for a time she was absorbed in what she was doing, but then she found herself thinking about how pleased her mother had been when she had first taken up the guitar, and how she had immediately arranged for Katy to have guitar lessons after school.

How awful that had been; she had simply hated learning classical guitar. The music was impossible to read, she disliked the teacher, loathed having to sit up straight and hold the guitar in a position that was completely alien to her own instincts, and worse still, detested being told she had to rest her foot on a ridiculous little foot stand. That was so outrageous. She smiled to herself at the thought of it. The upshot had been that within three weeks of starting, she had absolutely refused to play the guitar at all, until her mother had finally given up the idea. Why did parents always have to interfere? She didn't need sheet music; it was far easier to play by ear.

But today her heart really wasn't in it, and she just couldn't find some of the chords. After a few minutes of trying to remember the correct fingering, she became increasingly frustrated, ran the plectrum angrily across the strings and threw the guitar down on the bed.

She lay back, and surveyed her bedroom. For some

long-forgotten reason, every bit of the furniture in Katy's room had been painted apple-green. The bedside table, chest of drawers and wardrobe all sported matching thick coats of bright green paint, as though some fiendish decorator had grimly resolved to put every last drop to good use. The effect, now she considered it, was surprisingly unsatisfactory. Even the wallpaper had a green reoccurring pattern, and every time that she was confined to bed with a high temperature – usually due to recurrent bouts of tonsillitis – the green dots would dance about, playing tricks on her. Even now, as she stared at them, they seemed to move around.

Katy swivelled round onto her stomach and pressed her nose up against the small window, the metal frame of which stubbornly refused to shut securely. She peered out. The window only offered a view of the wall of the house next door, but if she leant precariously out she could just glimpse the back garden of their next-door neighbour. How odd it was that, despite living next to the family for over twelve years, her family had never actually met them? Why weren't her parents more sociable? Surely most families were at least on speaking terms with their neighbours. Yet the only time that she had even met the lady next door was when the cat had mysteriously disappeared, and Katy had decided to go round and ask all the neighbours to look for it in their garden sheds and garages. Come to think of it, she didn't even know the names of the people who lived on the adjoining side of their semi-detached house… and they shared a front garden.

There was an ash tree between the two houses which prevented much light from entering Katy's bedroom, but it was lovely to see its dancing branches reaching towards her like outstretched arms.

Katy vividly remembered suddenly waking up from a dream in the middle of the night, banging on the wall adjoining her mother's bedroom, shouting, 'Mummy, come here! There's a rabbit sitting in the branches of the tree and it's trying to get in through the bedroom window!'

Her mother had raced in, but couldn't see anything. 'There's nothing there, Katy. And anyway, rabbits can't climb trees, dear,' she had pointed out, rather annoyingly. But Katy was sure that she had seen it and refused to be consoled. She just knew it had been a rabbit.

She shivered at the thought, and watched the rain run down the panes of glass for a moment or two before drawing the green and white curtains and shutting out the night. She stretched out on her bed again, sighed deeply, and propped her head up against the pillows.

What a mess her room was! She could just hear her mother's voice: 'Katy, for goodness' sake, dear. If you don't want me to come into your room, you might at least make some effort yourself to keep it tidy. It's really not too much to ask is it?'

No, come to think of it, it was really quite a reasonable request. She would set to work and tidy up right now. She surveyed the clutter: her clothes were strewn about the room; the small green chair was completely immersed in a pile of once-worn jumpers, jeans and jackets; more sweaters were spilling out of drawers; and several odd socks lay around the floor. Her hockey stick and boots had been carelessly thrown against a teetering pile of 45's.

She began by carefully folding up her jumpers and

putting them away, then she hung up her jeans and jackets; next she put her crumpled clothes and worn socks into the dirty linen basket. She soon warmed to her task and, opening the drawer, took out a mass of random socks and began meticulously folding them into pairs, and then put them all away again. Excellent. This was going well.

The hockey stick was stashed next to her small telescope, behind the door. The boots were placed tidily in the bottom of the wardrobe. Only the records remained; they could go in alphabetical order along the wall. Why hadn't she done this before? Her room had never looked so tidy: her mother would be amazed at the transformation. What's more, there suddenly seemed to be so much more space.

Now she'd started, she might as well press on with her mission. The doors of the green toy cupboard were open, and since much of its contents had fallen out on the floor, she decided to turn her attention to reorganising it. Although the toy cupboard no longer actually contained any toys, and was now full of board games, a chemistry set and Katy's large and much-loved stamp collection, it was still known as such.

Katy arranged the boxes into neat piles, and replaced them tidily on the shelves. The stamp albums were stacked and the packs of cards sorted out. Feeling quite pleased with her efforts, Katy finally closed the cupboard doors, revealing a large hole in the faded green carpet in front of the cupboard, through which the bare floorboards could be clearly seen.

Katy could still detect a faintly acidic smell coming from the surrounding area. The hole marked the spot where one of the experiments, carried out using 'My First Chemistry Set', had gone spectacularly wrong.

A well-meaning aunt had given Katy the set for a birthday present, probably in the misguided belief that she would one day follow in her father's footsteps. But Katy soon found that the simple chemical tests suggested in the instructions were really boring, and thought she might pep up the scientific experiments by the addition of a few extra substances.

She'd tried pouring a little vinegar into a beaker of mixed chemicals, but nothing very exciting happened. What else could she add? Maybe some nail vanish remover? Nothing. Searching through the kitchen cupboard she came across some strong bleach and wondered whether that might liven things up. She'd just try adding a little bit.

No sooner had the bleach hit the mixture in the beaker, when the entire contents erupted with such force that the liquid spread itself over a wide area of Katy's bedroom, and green acrid gas filled the air. Katy, half choking, dropped the beaker in alarm and rushed out of the room to wash her hands and face. She tried hard to remove the evidence, but as she frantically wiped the liquid from the carpet, the fabric itself simply disintegrated.

That night the smell of chemicals was so awful that Katy slept with the window wide open. She managed to keep the hole in the carpet covered over for a long while before it finally came to her mother's notice. And she succeeded in half convincing her mother that it had simply appeared through the wear and tear of the cupboard door scraping against it. Although, thinking about it now, her mother must surely have guessed the truth all along.

Katy lay back on the bed. What an improvement! Now what should she do? But the minute she was no longer fully occupied, thoughts of the horrible letter that was burning a hole in her satchel downstairs returned, and she just couldn't keep her mind on anything else.

OK. Ways she could she avoid telling her mother...

Once again she let her imagination run away with her; this was always dangerous! What if there was a real fire at school tomorrow, and everyone got out safely, all thanks to Katy Warner for having the remarkable foresight to hold a practice run the previous day? She could see herself being called out to the front in assembly.

'Well done, Katy!' Dr Knight was saying. 'The whole school is deeply indebted to your immense prudence and outstanding organisational skills.'

'Katy! Katy! Katy!' Everyone would rise to their feet, clapping and cheering.

How proud her parents would be...

Or, better still, maybe the school would actually burn down during the night, and then no one would even care about the stupid fire practice and all her friends would also have to go to a different school... But this was pure fantasy; she was hardly going to start a real fire. She'd probably end up in a remand centre and bring shame on the family for ever. Katy forced herself back down to earth. Was she really going crazy?

Perhaps she should nip downstairs and help herself to another drink, since the first one or two seemed to have had no effect whatsoever. Or maybe she could just immerse herself in a book, and calm down; that would certainly take less effort.

The three shelves above the toy cupboard were crammed full of books. When she was younger she'd practically memorised all the *What Katy Did* books, and almost regarded the characters in them as role models. Now she was obsessed with Second World War escape stories. She could readily lose herself in the world of Spitfire pilots, and daring rescue missions. Yesterday she had almost missed supper as she was so absorbed in *Escape from Colditz*. She settled down again with the book, but try as she might, she just couldn't concentrate, and her thoughts were everywhere but on the story. She found herself re-reading several pages, and then completely lost her place. Finally she gave up, closed the book, and abandoned herself to daydreaming again.

The array of red, yellow and green rosettes which hung down the wall by the side of the bed caught her eye. A worrying thought occurred to her: maybe they wouldn't let her go riding again, after today's catastrophe. That would be terrible! Riding was her favourite pastime. Now they'd probably stop her helping out at the local stables.

They knew that mucking out, feeding the horses, and grooming their coats until they shone, was her idea of a perfect day; and how much she'd always wanted to have her own horse. It was so unfair that her parents wouldn't even consider it. But then, last summer, after incessant arguing and bargaining: triumph! She eventually persuaded her parents to allow her to go away on a week's riding holiday. She remembered how she'd so looked forward to it for weeks and weeks. Then, after three wonderful days' riding: disaster!

Katy re-ran the events in her mind. It was a beautiful sunny day and she was keen to improve her show jumping skills. Six riders had enrolled for a jumping lesson and they started off with some very low obstacles spaced around the field.

'Just trot round one behind the other and get the horses used to the idea of the jumps,' shouted the riding instructor. 'I'll tell each one of you when to go.'

They began to ride round one at a time, but as Katy waited for her turn, the horse immediately in front of her reared up onto its hind legs and the girl fell off. The young rider was unhurt and got up, but her horse cantered away.

Here's my big chance, thought Katy, and shouting, 'Don't worry, I'll catch it!' she and her horse galloped off, mane and tail flying out in the wind, chasing after the runaway horse. Katy felt like a cowboy, rounding up cattle in the Wild West. What she really needed was a lasso. Ever the heroine, and watched by the other riders, she bravely raced across the field. As the riderless horse slowed up, she managed to corner the frightened animal. Brilliant, she thought, I'll just try to grab its reins. And riding alongside it, she pulled her horse up sharply, leant out over the neck of the riderless horse and… that was all she remembered until she found herself lying on the ground groaning loudly as an intense pain shot up her leg.

She later found out that the startled animal had kicked out violently at Katy's horse, and she'd caught the full impact of its hoof on her leg. There were then two riderless horses cantering round unrestrained. The animals gradually came to a halt and began eating grass indifferently, some way away. But Katy continued to lie there, crying out in agony.

'For goodness' sake stop play-acting, Katy Warner. Get up!' shouted the instructor impatiently, not realising that she'd been hurt. 'You are just making matters worse!'

Despite the excruciating pain in her leg, Katy actually tried to stand up. The moment she put her weight on her right leg, the pain became unbearable. Her leg crumpled beneath her. She passed out.

The next event she dimly recalled was the loud ringing sound of an ambulance bell as it drove across the field to where she lay. Then, nothing.

Nothing at all, until she heard a voice calling her name. 'Katy! Katy, can you hear me?'

She opened her eyes and was amazed to see a nurse standing by her bed. Where on earth was she? Why was her right leg furnished with a magnificent full-leg plaster cast, and hoisted up in traction?

'Hello, Katy, I'm so glad you're awake at last. How are you feeling? I'm afraid you've fractured your leg. Don't worry, dear, we've notified your parents, and they'll be here soon.'

Katy gazed around the ward in disbelief. Everything seemed to be a varied shade of white. There was a strong smell of disinfectant. She felt rather sick and woozy and very sorry for herself.

So, this was the end of her dream holiday. And worse still, she wouldn't be able to walk for months. She remembered catching sight of her clothes on the chair next to her bed. There lay her much-loved leather riding boots and jodhpurs; they were ruined, cut right through to free her leg. That was the final straw. Katy burst into inconsolable tears.

After a week or so in hospital, Katy was transported home by ambulance. Eventually, she had to return to school. The local council thoughtfully arranged for her to be taken there by ambulance every day.

And then she became a star overnight! How she loved it! The daily arrival of the ambulance in the school playground was a much-heralded event. A small crowd would gather as she drew up. 'Here comes the ambulance!' 'Open the gates for Katy, please.' 'Don't stand there! Let Katy through!' 'Someone help her out.' 'Take her satchel, someone!'

Katy felt like royalty. Every one wanted to inscribe her plaster cast with a witty comment or an illustration, though of course only her closest friends were allowed to take turns in the playground with her crutches. It was brilliant.

Whole corridors of children had to be shepherded away to allow her to change classrooms whenever the bell rang. Going up and down the main wooden staircase in the school entrance hall was a major feat in itself. Katy smiled as she recalled how she graciously allowed one person to carry a crutch and another her satchel, while she held onto the banisters. She was even given a special place to sit during school assembly, and the staff were much more patient with her; a detention was out of the question as the ambulance was there to collect her at the end of each school day.

But then the ambulance gave way to a less exciting taxi, and finally her plaster cast was removed, and with it her celebrity status. All too soon school life reverted to its former battleground of pupil versus authority.

Sitting there now on her green eiderdown, Katy fervently wished that she could have remained such a celebrity. Now what a mess she was in.

She must think of something constructive to do. Should she start her homework or not? She felt, partly out of habit, that maybe she should get on with it, but what was the point? Would she ever actually hand it in?

She caught sight of a pair of blue eyes staring down at her reproachfully from the top of the wardrobe. They belonged to a very large plastic doll, which bore the inappropriate name of 'Baby Betty'. The doll had sat up there for as long as she could remember. Katy had emphatically stated that she hated dolls, but had anyone listened? Consequently, the accompanying changes of dolls' clothes had remained pristine in their original boxes and Katy had resolutely declared no interest in them whatsoever. Why wouldn't anyone take any notice when she had explained that what she really wanted most in the world was a Meccano set?

And for that matter, why hadn't she been born a boy? She'd always wanted to play football and absolutely hated wearing dresses. Life would have been so much more exciting. Instead she just didn't seem to fit in at all, and had to resign herself to the much less satisfactory role of tomboy.

Katy shivered. Why was this room so cold? She reached over and plugged in the convector heater. There was a faint burning smell, which gradually became stronger as the element heated up. Now she remembered:

the previous day she had accidentally set fire to a pair of stockings, which she had been attempting to dry… some of the charred fabric must have fallen onto the element. Her eyes began to water as the acrid smell intensified. She quickly switched the fire off again. Now she'd have to leave her room.

Passing her mother's room, she switched on the light, and glanced in. Maybe her mother had been taken ill again. Her mother did not enjoy very good health at the best of times. She'd better take a closer look.

The room was much larger than Katy's, and even colder. She could almost hear her mother's voice, complaining, 'My bedroom is like an ice-well!', and Katy had to admit that she had a point. No wonder her mother was so often in poor health. It was absolutely freezing in here. There was a small convector heater but it was completely unequal to the formidable task of producing enough heat to counteract the cold wind which battered unremittingly against the huge bay window. The old gas fire in the hearth had long ago ceased to work, serving only to produce a permanent, rather worrying, faint odour of unburned gas, which Katie noticed as soon as she walked through the door. It was sometimes so cold in this room that during the winter months Katy had seen frost on both the inside and outside of the windows.

She looked out at the streaming rain. Since the bedroom was built immediately above the lounge, the top of the huge horse chestnut tree outside surrounded the whole bay window, stretching out its long branches of dancing white catkins. They looked quite eerie, as the flower heads reflected the street light below.

Katy sat down on her mother's double bed. Even the orange nylon eiderdown had a cold, almost damp feel to it. Katy could quite understand why her mother had declared the bed to be so cold that she sometimes resorted to sleeping with a bolster down one side of it and her feet wrapped in a plastic bag, in an attempt to keep herself warm throughout the winter nights. Why did they have to live like this? It was ridiculous. Her father could well afford to have central heating installed.

She must have been at least twelve, Katy reflected, before it occurred to her that it was somewhat unusual for parents to have separate bedrooms. She could clearly remember showing her friends around the house, innocently explaining, 'This is my father's room, this is mine and here is my mother's bedroom.' What an odd family her friends must have thought them to be. She couldn't even recollect when the implications of these bizarre arrangements had finally dawned on her. How very naive she was!

There was no doubt in Katy's mind that much of her mother's ill health was caused by the stressful situation at home, and the aggravation she endured daily. As long as Katy could remember, her mother had suffered from a gastric ulcer, for she always took a variety of indigestion remedies, none of which really seemed to help. Her mother had to be quite careful about what type of food she ate, and she'd been advised to avoid anything that was too 'strong' or acidic, such as pickled cucumber, peppers or spicy food These, needless to say, were precisely the foods that her father loved to eat, having been brought up on a diet of pickled herrings, chopped liver, onions and red horseradish sauce.

Her mother smoked, her father did not. Her mother was teetotal; her father liked a drink. Her mother loved their cat; her father hated it and was allergic to its fur. Her father was very religious; her mother didn't believe in any of it. Her mother enjoyed visiting the West End of London; her father regarded driving into London as an ordeal to be avoided at all costs. In fact, there were few subjects which her parents ever agreed on. Why on earth had they ever got married at all? That remained a complete mystery.

She slowly surveyed the cheerless room. It was furnished throughout with heavy Art Deco furniture. The wardrobe, dressing table and chest of drawers were made of oak wood, but you couldn't fail to notice that the same bright apple-green paint that had been used so lavishly in Katy's bedroom had also found its way in here too, garishly adorning the built-in set of cupboards and bedside table.

Looking around the bedroom, Katy felt almost as though she was at a ballet exhibition. Every available space was adorned with numerous photographs and posters of Rudolph Nureyev and Margot Fonteyn. The bay window sill was crammed full with her mother's vast collection of ballet books.

How could anyone be so passionate about ballet? Katy wondered. Maybe it was an escape from the unhappy life she led. It was certainly an all-absorbing obsession; a magical world in which her mother seemed to utterly lose herself. Katy gazed at the mountain of programmes from Covent Garden, stretching back at least ten years, stacked up next to the bed. Her mother had tried so hard to share her great love of ballet with her, so why was she unable to appreciate it all? She had to admit that the more ballet performances she'd been reluctantly taken to, the less she had enjoyed the experience. She really must be quite a disappointment to her mother, she told herself savagely.

But then her mother took things too far. How could she think nothing of spending the night before the new booking period opened, sleeping on the pavement in a queue outside Covent Garden Opera House? That was an outrageous way to behave, and she had been right to try and stop her: 'Mummy, you're surely not going to sleep in the street. It's ridiculous at your age!'

'Look dear, it's all arranged. You know it's the only way I can afford to buy tickets for the next season.'

'But how can you possibly sleep on the pavement? What if it rains? Can't someone else get the tickets for you? It's not even safe!'

'It is perfectly safe, dear, and we are very well organised. We can shelter under the awnings, and we've even arranged to buy breakfast at the kiosk in Floral Street. Besides, I really enjoy the camaraderie.'

And that was that. And so successful had it been that now it was an annual event. It was a good job her father didn't know about it!

Katy stretched and stood up. She looked carefully at the dressing table. Were there any clues here? She saw that her mother's silver brush and comb set had been left out, and three sets of earrings were lying in the cut class tray. Several of the drawers were open, and a silk scarf spilled out onto the floor. Yes, it was likely that her mother had been changing to go out for yet another evening at the ballet, and had left the house in rather a hurry. She'd probably made an unscheduled trip into London; maybe she'd been offered a ticket to see a last-minute change of cast at the Opera House. That would certainly be an event not to be missed!

Katy sighed. The rain continued to lash unremittingly at the windows. What a depressing room this was. She could stand it no longer. She was becoming more and more despondent. Pull yourself together, she told herself sharply, it's all too easy to wallow in a sea of self-pity.

She turned, switched off the light and left the room abruptly, closing the door resolutely behind her. With a sudden urge she almost threw herself down the stairs, recklessly skipping the last six and landing with a crash in the hall.

CHAPTER 6

Katy picked herself up. No damage done! Right, where had she left her satchel?

There it was, lying abandoned on the kitchen floor. She rescued it, and putting the green baize tablecloth on the dining room table, tipped out the contents.

A pile of schoolbooks tumbled out, followed by a pencil case, a hairbrush, a blackened banana, some Liquorice Allsorts which had long parted company with their bag, a Caramac bar and a bag of wet swimming things. Finally, from the bottom of the bag, her blue school cardigan emerged. Katy gratefully put it on.

For a while Katy tried hard to ignore the fact that next to the heap of books lay the fateful white envelope which had been haunting her innermost thoughts. She sat and gazed at it for several minutes, then tentatively turned it over. It was boldly marked:

STRICTLY PRIVATE AND CONFIDENTIAL
Dr and Mrs R. Warner

Katy felt an irresistible urge to rip it into tiny pieces and bury the whole lot in the dustbin. That would make her feel so much better. But what would it achieve? She still wouldn't be able to go to school, and there was no doubt that Mr Knight would soon be on the phone again.

She sat back in the chair, sighed deeply and stared into space. If only there was someone she could talk to now… maybe she was ready to unburden herself at last. She tried to rehearse the conversation with her mother in her head, but all she could think about was how utterly devastated her mother would be. She could just imagine those reproachful eyes gazing into her own.

Katy's mind kept racing ahead of her: the meeting between her bewildered parents and Mr Knight… the revelations of her previous suspensions, when she'd had to pretend to go to school for a week… all those letters home which hadn't been delivered. It was too frightening even to contemplate. She felt really sick.

It had all seemed a clever game, an innocent diversion. Now it had all spiralled out of control. How could she have been so incredibly stupid?

Katy noticed with surprise that her hand holding the letter was shaking. What was the matter with her? She must calm down a bit. Absentmindedly she ate several of the Liquorice Allsorts.

Suddenly, she couldn't bear the sight of the envelope for a minute longer, and returned it to her school bag, impulsively throwing everything else back on top. She must put it out of her mind or she'd really go mad. But how on earth would she be able to sleep tonight with all this hanging over her?

Why was it that school seemed to be just one long drawn out battlefield? And who on earth was misguided enough to think that schooldays are the happiest days of anyone's life?

Perhaps she was a bit resentful of authority at times, and maybe she was one of the most frequent visitors to the Headmaster's study, but at least her parents hadn't been involved so far. They were blissfully unaware that she'd spent so much of her school time either kept in school for a detention, or else sent home (when she would either while away time on the swings in the park, or else go for a bus ride).

Luckily the school never seemed to follow anything up, but there had been one unfortunate incident when she had been staying with her best friend, Madeleine. It had all started, she recalled, when she'd returned home from school one day to find the house in darkness.

'Anyone at home?' she shouted.

'Katy, I'm so glad you're back,' was the faint reply. 'I'm upstairs.'

Katy ran up to her mother's room and found her doubled up on the bed, in great pain. 'I've been very sick, Katy, and I feel really unwell. Do you think you could call Dr Elliman, dear?'

Katy phoned the doctor, who arrived half an hour later. After only a few minutes he told her, 'Your mother needs to go into hospital, Katy. I'm going to phone for an ambulance now!'

Katy was shocked to see the ambulance pull up outside their house and to watch her mother being taken downstairs on a stretcher by two medics. She stood in the hall feeling completely helpless.

'Can I go with her, please?' she asked the doctor.

'Yes, of course you should go with her, and you need to be very sensible and pack a bag with a nightie and her washing things and anything else you think she might need. Be very quick, Katy'

Katy rushed round the house, and only just remembered to take the front door key with her. Her poor mother; she looked so awful! Why hadn't she come home from school earlier? Her mother must have been lying there in pain for ages. Why hadn't she taken more care of her? What if she were to die?

Her mother was admitted to the local hospital and Katy was very alarmed to be told that her mother's stomach ulcer had suddenly flared up again, which meant that she would need an immediate operation. Since Katy's father had, not altogether unsurprisingly, announced that he was absolutely unable to change his weekly appointments in Birmingham and would therefore also be away, it was arranged that Katy should stay with her best friend Madeleine for a few days.

Great! Although she was worried about her mother's operation, at last she'd get to stay at Madeleine's. It was something that she'd always wanted to do.

She could see Madeleine's house from the upstairs window of her father's bedroom, and their garage, at the end of the back garden, had a steep drive leading to the next road, right next to Madeleine's house.

Katy could vividly remember meeting Madeleine on the very first day they had moved into their house, and how they'd looked shyly over the fence at each other. Both aged five, they had been very excited to discover that they'd be starting at the same infant school the following week. From that day onwards, they remained firm friends. But although they saw each other every day, Katy had never stayed at Madeleine's overnight; and now she was staying until the weekend.

Unfortunately, on the third day of her stay with Madeleine's family, Katy had an accident during a chemistry practical at school. She knocked a over a conical flask full of potassium permanganate solution which rolled off the bench and smashed into several pieces on the floor, covering the skirt and stockings of her partner Jane with bright purple splashes of liquid.

The class cheered and started to clap and shout, 'Nice one, Katy!'

'Dear, oh dear! What's happened now?' cried a flustered Dr Fry, hurrying across the lab to see for himself. 'What on earth do you think you are doing, Katy Warner? Can't you be more careful?' He gazed anxiously at the ever-expanding large puddle of mauve liquid and broken glass which lay on the floor.

Katy rushed over to help, and grabbing the floor cloth out of the sink, tried to wipe Jane's skirt with it, but only succeeded in making it even worse as the cloth itself was far from clean.

'Just leave it now, please, Katy!' shouted Dr Fry, beginning to panic. 'For goodness' sake, Jane, go and wash your legs at once! Do you have another skirt you could change into?'

'Yes, sir, my PE skirt,' said Jane and hastily left the laboratory.

'Katy, get some paper towels and a dust pan and brush. Now!'

Everyone left their benches and gathered round to look.

'Kindly return to your places, everyone. Katy, if you just took more care you wouldn't cause so much trouble!'

Katy began to clear up the mess. The accusations were ridiculous. It had been an accident; Jane was her friend. Of course she was really sorry that her friend's skirt was ruined.

'I didn't do it on purpose, sir. I was just—'

'Yeah, it was an accident, sir,' chorused the others, treading in the broken glass.

'For heaven's sake, everyone, stand back! Can one of you go and fetch the technician?'

Katy's hands were fast turning bright mauve.

'Katy, go and wash your hands, straight away. And you will of course have to pay for the broken flask.'

'Why will I have to pay for it?' argued Katy, ineffectively trying to wring the mauve paper towels into the sink. 'We only have to pay for *deliberate* breakages. I've told you, it was just an accident.'

'Don't argue with me. If you want to argue you can go and see the Headmaster,' snapped Dr Fry, keen to be seen to be once more in control of the situation.

'Well, that's just not fair and I'm *not* paying!' protested Katy, getting more upset by the minute, as she noticed that the sleeves of her school blouse were now also stained with splashes of violet.

The technician had meanwhile appeared, bringing rubber gloves and a sponge and bucket.

'Katy, kindly leave the clearing up to Barbara. Go and wash yourself immediately, and then you can go and explain what happened to Mr Knight!'

So it was that Katy was ordered to apologise to Dr Fry for her lack of self-control, and was further informed that since the school could not tolerate such 'flagrant insubordination', she was being sent home 'forthwith'. A letter and an invoice for a replacement conical flask would immediately be posted to her parents.

Boiling over with resentment at such unfair treatment, Katy stormed across the school playground, watched by the Headmaster, and flounced out of the school gates. She marched up the road, but as she turned the corner it suddenly occurred to her that it was only eleven o'clock in the morning, and she had absolutely nowhere to go. She slowed up, feeling somewhat less confident. What should she do now?

She considered the matter: her house was locked up since her parents were away, and only Madeleine's mother had the key. She couldn't climb in, since all the windows were closed. Where could she go all day? It would obviously be better to just while away the rest of the day and arrive back at her friend's house at the normal time, saying nothing of the day's events. Anyway, since both of Madeleine's parents were out at work all day, she couldn't go there even if she wanted to.

She wandered slowly up to the High Road. Just as she reached the bus stop a bus drew up, and on a whim she jumped on. She was surprised at her own wild decision, but the choice of where to get off was made for her, since it was only going as far as East Finchley station. What now? The bus stopped right outside the Tube station. She might as well catch a train.

She bought a ticket to London and got on the first train

that arrived. But thinking that London was probably a bit too far to go, and seeing that the train was approaching Highgate station, she decided to get off. Yes, a walk in the woods would be an excellent way to pass the day.

It was a good decision. The autumn sun was shining and Katy felt at one with the world as she walked happily along the path, listening to the birds singing. She kicked the leaves about in the wind and strode confidently along for some time, managing to forget all her worries. Gradually her thoughts centred on the fact that she was really quite hungry, and seeing a park bench in the clearing, she sat down. It must be nearly lunchtime; she might as well eat here.

Katy opened her satchel and took out the packed lunch that had been prepared for her by Madeleine's mother. The sandwiches were egg – her favourite – and there was a bottle of lemonade, an apple and a large slice of chocolate cake. This was brilliant. Squirrels ran along the branches of the trees, and the rustling leaves looked so lovely in their deep reds and yellows. It was so much better than sitting in (or in her case, standing outside), a double maths lesson.

If only her friends could see her now. Actually, she had to admit to herself, it would be even nicer if she could share this adventure with them… but it was really no good feeling lonely. Instead she shared her lunch with some cheeky pigeons that had joined her. But soon she was surrounded by dozens of them and she had to stand up and clap her hands to get rid of them all.

Looking at her watch, she saw that it was still only half past two. What should she do next? Since she didn't want to return to Madeleine's house before four-thirty, she might as well waste a bit more of the day here. She walked along aimlessly for some time, wandering further into the woods, lost in thought… how very unfair of Mr Knight not to listen to her point of view. Jane's mother would have understood about the spoilt skirt. Of course it was just an accident, they must all have realised that. Why had things got out of hand so quickly? It was all so unfair. No one else would have been sent home for such a trifling matter.

She walked deeper into the woods, and eventually became aware that the sun was now quite low down in the sky and the shadows were beginning to lengthen. It was probably about time to think about finding her way home.

Katy began to search for a path leading out of the woods but found that she had absolutely no idea which direction to take. The best way to find the way out, logically, would be to stay on one path and just keep walking in what seemed to be a straight line. This she did, quickening her pace somewhat, but was alarmed to find that the track that she was following became very narrow and muddy. Her feet were slipping as she walked; this was certainly not the right footpath. But she had decided to walk in a straight line, and nothing was going to stop her! She soon had to force her way between thick bushes and small saplings, which were twisted together to form an almost impassable barrier of undergrowth. It was so gloomy that she kept tripping over unseen brambles. 'Ow, that really hurt!' she said aloud, as a holly bush scratched her across the face, but she continued squeezing herself through the foliage until she could go no further.

What on earth was she doing here? She was in the

middle of a dense thicket. The wind had increased, showering large red maple leaves and little wings of sycamore seeds down on her. 'This is awful! I'm never ever going to get out of here,' she heard her own voice say, but it sounded flat and empty in the silence. How could a dropped flask in a Chemistry lesson have led to this? There was no alternative but to go back the way she had come. But where was that?

Suddenly a pigeon flew out of the tree in front of her with a great flurry of wings. Katy jumped in fright. You're being ridiculous; it's only a bird, she told herself. For goodness' sake calm down and find the path again. She fought her way out of the thicket and eventually found herself in a clearing, where the forest floor was covered in acorns. She could just make out a path veering away through the trees. It was certainly worth following it; she must be near the edge of the forest.

After a while she became aware of the crack of broken twigs. There was definitely someone behind her. If she let the person catch her up, she could ask them for directions of the woods. She stopped. The footsteps stopped too and the woods were suddenly ominously silent again. Well, she couldn't wait forever; it was probably just some children playing a game. She continued along the path. The rustle behind her began again. Katy turned round and stood still. There was no one there. Total silence.

Suddenly, from behind a tree, a figure appeared in the darkness. Katy gasped. She tried to yell out, but although her lips moved, no sound came out of her mouth. Her heart seemed to have forgotten how to beat. An icy fear crept over her. He was going attack her; she was sure.

Run! Just run! Why couldn't she? She seemed to be momentarily transfixed to the spot. She became acutely aware of her own breathing. The man stood equally motionless, staring at her. His hair was matted and his clothes dishevelled. Katy noticed that his trousers were tied up with string. The tramp lurched towards her. His breath reeked of alcohol. Katy reeled away from him as he tried to grab her arm. His hands were absolutely filthy.

'Don't be frightened little girl,' he burbled drunkenly. 'I promise I won't hurt you. Here, have a drink!' With his other hand, he produced a bottle from a brown paper bag in his torn coat pocket. He thrust it threateningly into Katy's fearful face.

Katy, gripped by panic, heard herself scream piercingly. Instinctively she pulled her arm away sharply from his grip and the tramp, startled by the noise, let go of her sleeve and staggered backwards. Forcing her unwilling legs to work, Katy ran back down the path as fast as she could. She had absolutely no idea where she was going. Ignoring the stabbing pain in her side, she raced along wildly. Darkness was really beginning to close in and it was increasingly difficult to follow the footpaths at all. She was completely lost.

Where was the path?

Was the tramp still following her?

Exhausted, she tripped over a half-buried log and fell heavily, grazing both knees. She lay completely motionless on the damp forest floor, the blood pounding in her head. Clutching her satchel as if it might bring her some sort of comfort, she fought back the tears. The woods were so gloomy and menacing; the thought of having to spend the night alone there terrified her.

From nowhere, a large black dog suddenly bounded across to her, wagging its tail enthusiastically and barking loudly. It gazed at her for a moment with deep brown eyes, and then raced away again as suddenly as it had arrived. Minutes later, still barking madly, it returned excitedly to Katy's side and stood next to Katy panting vigorously. She could feel its warm breathe against her face. Half sitting up, she reached out to stroke it and saw that this time it had brought its owners, as a middle-aged couple, who had evidently been enjoying an evening stroll, appeared from the gloom. They were clearly very surprised to find a girl in mauve-spattered school uniform lying there all alone, evidently very close to tears.

'You poor thing!' exclaimed the lady sympathetically. 'Do let me help you up.' The dog continued to bark noisily. 'Good boy, Charlie. Quieten down now.'

Katy was so relieved by their arrival that she immediately put on a brave face and tried to make light of the situation. She managed to scramble to her feet.

'Oh, I'm all right, thank you. I was trying to take a short cut on the way to the station, when I tripped over. I think I've grazed my knee a bit,' she explained rather unconvincingly. She felt a complete idiot. What must they think? How could she have panicked like that?

The couple were very understanding. The lady carefully wiped Katy's grazed knees and insisted that they accompany her all the way back to the Tube station. 'It's so easy to get lost in these woods; luckily Charlie always knows his way home. It's quite tricky to find the station from here, but we'll show you the way. We're going in that direction in any case.'

The station turned out to be even further away than Katy had thought, and when they finally arrived the lady had insisted on making sure she'd bought the right train ticket. Such a kind lady! Katy's faith in mankind was almost restored.

When Katy finally arrived back at her friend's house it was well after eight o'clock. She felt very apprehensive as she knocked on the door. Madeleine's mother opened it.

'Katy! Thank goodness! It's Katy. She's here!' she shouted, and gave Katy a passionate hug. To Katy's immense surprise, she looked as if she was about to burst into tears. Why was she so upset?

'Oh Katy, where on earth have you been? We were all so worried. I telephoned your school and the secretary said that you had left at eleven o'clock this morning! What ever happened to you?'

'I'm really sorry, Auntie Trudy' said Katy, 'I didn't mean to be so late, I just got—' but her friend's mother interrupted her.

'There's been a full-scale search, Katy, I even called the police! I must tell them that you are here now.' And she rushed back into the house to telephone.

Katy was so shocked that the colour drained from her face. The police! What terrible trouble was she in now?

CHAPTER 7

Madeleine came racing down the stairs. 'Hi Katy. You look like you've seen a ghost! Are you OK?'

'Yeah. I'm fine,' said Katy 'Just a bit tired.'

'So where on earth did you go then? What's happened to you?'

Just then Madeleine's parents returned. 'You two can chat in a minute. Katy, come into the kitchen, please. We want to talk to you first,' said Madeleine's mother.

Katy wondered what on earth they must be thinking. Her legs were scratched and bleeding and she had two large plasters on her knee. Her gymslip and blazer were covered in mud and her blouse was spattered with mauve blotches. She couldn't even imagine what her hair must look like. Sitting one side of the kitchen table, with Madeleine's parents opposite, looking extremely grave, she was afraid that this was going to be a really difficult discussion.

Madeleine's father would be OK. Although he looked quite stern and had been a Major in the British Army, fighting out in Burma during the war, Katy knew that he always had a soft spot for her. But she was only too aware that Madeleine's mother regarded her as a potential troublemaker.

'I'm so sorry for causing you all this trouble, Aunty Trudy,' said Katy, wondering just how much they already knew. 'I was sent home from school this morning, but I didn't have the key, so I just thought I'd just go for a bus ride and come back when you got home.'

'You look as though you've been for more than just a bus ride!' said Madeleine's mother grimly. There was a silence. 'So exactly where have you been for the last nine hours?'

'Well I didn't mean to, but I went for a walk in Highgate woods and then I got a bit lost,' said Katy, rather lamely.

'In the woods! You spent the day on your own in the woods? Katy, don't you think that was a very irresponsible thing to do? Don't you realise how dangerous it can be for a girl alone in the woods?'

'I didn't *mean* to spend all day there, only to eat my lunch. I'm very sorry.'

Katy was surprised how upset Auntie Trudy was. She made an instant decision: she definitely wouldn't mention the tramp!

'Katy, I'm afraid we've had to let your mother know that you were missing. You know perfectly well that she is recovering from a serious operation. The last thing she needs at a time like this is to be worried by your ridiculous escapades. You have really been so thoughtless. And you do realise that *we* are responsible for you, Katy?'

Katy was upset. Of course she hadn't wanted to cause her mother any anxiety. It was ridiculous to even suggest it. She hadn't *planned* to get lost. She began to feel very sorry for herself. If only they knew what *she'd* been through.

'Katy, what have you to say?'

'I'm really so sorry. Please phone the hospital and tell her I'm OK.'

Madeleine's father spoke for the first time. 'Well, Katy, you might be interested to know that I telephoned your Headmaster,' he said, with a twinkle in his eye. 'Told him just what I thought of him! Fancy sending a young girl home without first checking that there was someone there. Didn't take it very well, I can tell you. The police interviewed him too.' And, unseen by his wife, he winked at Katy.

Katy cheered up immediately on hearing this surprising piece of news. To think that someone had stood up for her this time, and had actually questioned the authority of the Headmaster! If only she'd been there to see the look on his face when the police arrived at the school. They must have driven into the car park in a marked police car. She could just imagine the scene in his office…

Her reverie was sharply interrupted by Auntie Trudy. 'Right, Katy. You look as though you're in a trance. Go upstairs and have a bath and wash your hair. Leave me all those dirty clothes to wash. I'll have a cup of tea and some toast ready for you when you come down.'

And that was the end of the matter. It was never mentioned again during the rest of her stay.

If only Uncle Jack was here now. He'd know what to do.

Katy tried to push the events of the present day to the back of her mind and began to focus her thoughts on the homework which had been set, although she knew it was extremely unlikely that she would ever actually be handing it in.

She picked up her satchel. Where was her homework diary? There it was, under the bag of swimming things. What subjects were there tonight? Only two things due in the following day: French and maths. She'd do the French. It was very straightforward: just answering a few questions on a passage from the text book which they had read in class, earlier that day. It was odd, she mused, she really liked learning French and found it easy to read, and she could remember new vocabulary without really trying. So why didn't this ability make Mr Frapp, the French teacher, friendlier towards her? Instead it only seemed make him even more antagonistic. You just couldn't win.

He knew full well that she hated being called 'Kathleen', and that no one ever used that name. It was worse than being harassed by her classmates; at least she could retaliate with them. Today's exchange had been totally ridiculous: 'À *quelle heure avez-vous fini vos devoirs?*' Mr Frapp had asked the class.

No one put their hand up.

'*Kathleen, à quelle heure avez-vous fini vos devoirs?*'

Katy knew full well that he'd asked her what time she finished her homework, and she could easily have replied, '*J'ai fini mes devoirs à huit heures et demie, Monsieur*', but because he called her Kathleen, she blanked him.

There was a silence. The class waited expectantly.

'*Kathleen,* à *quelle heure avez-vous fini vos devoirs?*' he repeated very loudly and slowly.

Katy defiantly stared at the floor in front of her.

Mr Frapp pushed his chair back very deliberately and stood up. Katy wondered how long she dared to ignore him. She knew he was slowly approaching her desk. He stood next to her for a moment and then picked up her French textbook. This was a battle of wills.

Suddenly she felt a sharp pain on the side of her ear as the textbook made an unexpectedly violent impact with her head. Mr Frapp repeated the question a third time. This time, Katy indignantly supplied the required answer. Mr Frapp returned to his desk and continued as if nothing had happened. Similar infantile battles were re-enacted unfailingly in every French lesson, much to Katy's aggravation and the enjoyment of the rest of the class; and the more she protested, the more he would persist. Well she wouldn't bother to do his stupid homework. And returning the books to her satchel, she glanced at the maths.

Maths lessons were always a fiasco and the tables were decidedly turned in favour of the pupils. Katy often felt very sorry for the hapless maths teacher, who was very young and inexperienced and had little self-confidence. Right from the start the class had immediately sensed his nervousness and, acting almost as a pack, proceeded to exploit his weaknesses mercilessly. Students wandered around the classroom, refusing to sit down. Many openly worked on various other subjects, which had been set for homework. The poor man was virtually unable to keep any semblance of order during his lessons and had, on more than one occasion, actually been reduced to tears. Today two of the boys had got their packed lunches out and started to eat their sandwiches in open defiance.

The noise was such that Mr Knight suddenly appeared in the doorway, and stood there, resplendent in his black gown. Complete silence followed his arrival. Everyone shuffled to their feet. Even the teacher, Mr Remington, looked terrified.

'Is this how you treat my members of staff?' boomed the Headmaster. No one moved. 'Return to your desks forthwith! Any student who sees fit to eat or drink during this lesson, or indeed any lesson, will spend their entire lunch break running circuits round the school track. Be very clear about that.'

Everybody rapidly returned to their places. 'I am minded to keep the whole class behind in detention. Can anyone suggest why I should not do so?' There was no reply. He glared at the class. 'You will address members of my staff with respect at all times. What have you got to say to Mr Remington?'

'Sorry, sir,' chorused the class.

'You were able to produce more noise than that when I came in.'

'*Sorry, sir!*' the class bellowed.

Mr Knight stood there for a further minute, then said, 'Thank you, Mr Remington. Please carry on!' and swept out of the room.

They watched as Mr Remington tried to pull himself together. He looked as though he was sure that this must surely spell the end of his teaching career. He glanced at his watch: only twenty minutes to go.

Taking a deep breath, he announced rather shakily, 'Right, class, please continue with the exercise on page twenty-four, in silence.' And since for once there were no dissenting voices, he added more forcefully, 'Anyone talking will be punished.' No one argued with him.

Mr Remington had devised a unique method of punishment. It was similar to giving out 'lines', but instead he made the troublemakers copy out pages and pages of square root tables, from their books of tables. These were to be handed in to him during the following maths lesson. Even this form of punishment was doomed to failure, since the members of class who were sitting in the front row would surreptitiously steal the impositions back from his desk, as soon as his back was turned. The pages of tables then became a much-sought-after currency and were swiftly sold on to the next person who was to be punished. Mr Remington never seemed to notice that he was receiving the same pieces of work several times over.

Since Katy had already purchased the quota of four pages of tables which had been meted out to her that day, she turned to the homework: two pages of quadratic equations. She could remember absolutely nothing about this topic. She must have been daydreaming when they'd got to that chapter. Never mind, she'd leave it until the following morning when, if necessary, she could always consult her friends.

The clock chimed. It was half past seven. Katy was very tempted to go and cook something to eat, but then remembered that she hadn't finished practising the Mozart sonata. The exam was only a week away; she might as well do something useful. She went back into the lounge and sat down again at the piano.

Piano exams were *so* stressful. The last one had been a real nightmare. How nervous she'd been. A cold bolt of fear hit her the minute she entered the vast examination room. Sitting down at the unfamiliar grand piano, she felt almost paralysed and completely messed up the first piece, although she knew it backwards. She stopped half way through, turned round to the examiner and started to apologise; she'd better give up… she'd forgotten the piece…

But the examiner was very understanding about it. 'It's all right, Katy. Just relax, and start again in your own time. Lots of people tense up in exams. Don't worry, you'll be fine.'

And she was. She started again, and somehow managed to get into 'automatic-pilot' mode; her hands knew the notes but she was aware that if she actually tried to think about what she was playing or stopped, she'd be lost again. And her hands just took over! It was such a strange phenomenon, goodness only knows how it worked; it just did. The only problem was the sight-reading; never her strong point. So, all in all, it was truly amazing to find that she had actually gained a Merit in the Grade 6 piano exam; she'd been so sure that she'd failed.

And now she'd have to go through it all over again. Why? Who cared what piano exams you passed? What was the point of exams, anyway? Surely you either enjoyed playing, or you didn't.

One of the worst things about learning the piano was being asked to perform for her mother's friends. Her mother must know by now that she hated it. Surely she was well aware that if Katy was forced to play, she would do so with such extreme reluctance and bad grace that the resulting performance scarcely merited the trouble.

Oh well, she might as well practise for Grade 7. At least no one was here to listen. Where was her music case?

Katy smiled to herself as she remembered the journey she made to her last piano lesson. The lengths she went to go in order to spice up her life were really ridiculous. Piano lessons were every Tuesday evening after school, and the journey to the teacher's house necessitated a tedious walk of a mile and a half. But by taking a short cut through the recreation ground, she could easily knock a good ten minutes from the journey time. Needless to say, Katy's mother had expressly forbidden this route.

Although the short cut was much used during the day, few ventured there at night because the pathway was entirely unlit; but as far as Katy was concerned, the walk through the recreation grounds at night was the only exciting part of going to piano lessons at all. As she arrived at the gates of the park, Katy would dare herself to walk through. Should she, or shouldn't she?

This Tuesday she had hesitated and walked straight past the gates. But, not wanting to take the coward's way out, she decided she must prove herself and she turned back and followed the narrow pathway beside the small brook. The path was partially obscured on one side by a row of trees behind which was a series of air raid shelter bunkers, much favoured by courting couples. She set off at a fast pace, and as the lights from the road faded, her eyes gradually became accustomed to the darkness. As she strode along she wondered if other teenagers deliberately took unnecessary risks; maybe it was necessary, since everyday life was just so boring.

Quickening her pace a little more she was quite relieved to reach the point where she could see the faint glow of the streetlights at the other end of the path. Only another five minutes. She slowed down a bit. She'd done it! She emerged unscathed, but then arrived at the lesson ten minutes earlier than expected, and had to sit and wait for the preceding lesson to finish. What had been the point of that?

Katy opened her music. In a thin wobbly script, Miss Rawlings had scrawled some faint words in pencil. With great difficulty Katy managed to decipher them as, 'Check fingering. Keep a steady beat.' She could just imagine the shaky hand writing it.

Miss Rawlings lived in a decrepit bungalow surrounded by an overgrown garden with huge bushes and rampantly rambling roses. The thorny brambles were like tentacles ensnaring any unsuspecting visitor trying to negotiate the semi-hidden path leading to the front door.

After prolonged knocking at the door, the old lady would eventually appear, her hair tied up in a bun. Often she seemed rather surprised, mumbling, 'Oh, hello dear, I didn't know that you were coming today. Do come through.' Katy suspected that she probably greeted everyone with those words.

The cottage itself evidently dated from well before the war, and as such, had remained entirely unchanged; years of dust and grime covered all its surfaces. But the most unpleasant aspect of entering the bungalow was the fact that an inexplicably strong smell of overcooked sprouts pervaded every room. Katy could almost smell the awful stench now as she sat in front of her music.

Poor Miss Rawlins. Katy felt quite sorry for her; she was so thin and frail. Even in the summer she wore several moth-eaten woollen cardigans, one over the other, an old worn skirt and thick, dark brown wrinkled stockings. You couldn't help noticing that her fingers were bent with arthritis. Maybe she had once been a skilled pianist, though Katy couldn't imagine it. The fact that she managed to play the piano at all, wearing fingerless woollen gloves, was a miracle.

It always seemed to Katy that the house was entirely overrun with cats. Wherever you went, there were bowls of half-eaten cat food and litter trays filled with pieces of newspaper. She had a sudden vision of finding Miss Rawlings lying lifeless on the floor, surrounded by a pack of hungry felines. And how long would she lie there before someone found eventually discovered her body?

Over the years, Katy had been taught by a succession of rather odd piano teachers. The worst of all, as far as she was concerned, was a creepy, slimy, fish-like weasel-faced young man who had preceded Miss Rawlins. Katy's mother had spotted him playing the piano to the customers (mostly admiring housewives) in the local tea rooms. Since he owned a car, he was able given Katy piano lessons at her home, and she knew her mother had been rather proud to secure the services of such a distinguished musical exponent.

Katy however, thoroughly disliked him from the start. She particularly loathed the way he always sat close up to her on the double piano stool while she played. She shuddered to remember how once, while showing her the finer points of expressiveness when playing a repetitive phrase of *Für Elise*, which he had assured her should sound like the words 'I love you', he had passionately kissed her full on the lips. It was totally repulsive. Katy was so disgusted that she immediately related the details of this surprising and distasteful episode to her best friend Madeleine.

Evidently, Madeleine relayed the tale to others too, since within the week the piano teacher suddenly disappeared in mysterious circumstances, to be replaced by the present elderly retired spinster. (No reasons were ever offered to explain his peremptory dismissal, and the matter was never referred to.) Not long after this incident, a smart young lady was evidently deemed to be a more appropriate pianist at the tea rooms, and the young man was replaced there too. The middle-aged female clientele promptly also left in droves.

Katy removed the red cover from the piano keys and began to practise a few warm-up scales and arpeggios. She rubbed her hands, but it was so cold that her fingers just wouldn't move fast enough. She'd have to go upstairs and change into some warmer clothes.

She was nearly at the top of the stairs when the telephone began to ring again, its insistent clatter reverberating along the landing. Racing up the last few stairs she dived into her father's office at the end of the landing to answer the phone.

CHAPTER 8

The old black Bakelite telephone was almost buried under piles of letters and papers on her father's desk.

Perched on her father's vast leather swivel chair, Katy made a grab for the receiver.

'Hi, it's me,' said the familiar voice of her friend Madeleine. 'What are you doing tonight?'

'Nothing in particular,' replied Katy, 'I'm on my own here.'

'Yeah, I know. I think that your mother and mine have gone into London together. How do you fancy going up to the West End again?'

'I suppose we could,' agreed Katy slowly, 'but we don't know what time they'll be back, and anyway it's absolutely pouring with rain...'

'I'm certain that they won't be back till late. It'll be OK. Come on, Katy, let's do it. It was so exciting last time!'

Katy was so fed up that she couldn't be bothered either to change into smart clothes or to travel into London. She just wasn't in the mood. 'Look, I haven't eaten yet...'

'That's all right, we can get a coffee and sandwich in town. It'll save you the trouble of cooking.'

'Actually, I've had such a rubbish day at school today that I really don't feel like going anywhere just now.'

'But you're always having bad days at school,' objected her friend. 'And besides, you'd forget about your day once we went out.'

Katy hesitated. She'd have to tell someone sooner or later.

There were no curtains in the study and a big black fly kept buzzing frantically against the windows trying to get out. She sat and watched its fruitless efforts. Finally, she replied, 'Yes, but this time it's been really bad… and guess what?'

'What?'

Katy took a deep breath. 'I'm actually being expelled!'

There was a silence on the other end of the phone. And then, 'Gosh, so what happened, then?'

Katy explained about the fire practice and the small boy. It sounded absolutely ridiculous, she had to admit. What on earth had made her think she would get away with such a stupid plan?

Madeleine listened sympathetically. 'Well it sounds like a pretty brilliant day to me! Don't worry about getting chucked out, there're lots of other schools you can go to. You could even come to my school.'

Madeleine went to a private school. There was absolutely no chance that Katy's father would pay for her to go there, especially after this.

'Anyway, maybe they'll change their minds,' added Madeleine.

'I don't think there's much chance of that,' said Katy quietly.

'Well, look, think about it. If you do want to go out later, give me a ring back,' persisted Madeleine.

'OK. Bye then.'

'Bye.' Even her best friend didn't seem to understand the way she felt.

Katy swung round and round on the swivel chair, wondering what to do. She looked at the huge black wooden cupboard, stuffed full with piles of old papers, which had spilled out into heaps on the threadbare carpet. Folders, files and letters lay all round the room. How could anyone ever work in this mess?

The office was actually the same size as her bedroom but it appeared very small and cramped. A huge glass-fronted bookcase entirely filled the opposite wall. It was piled to the ceiling with papers, journals and books. On the top shelf, covered in dust, was an array of samples of metal plates in various stages of rust, and bundles of metallic strips which had once been the subject of scientific tests, having been dipped in various rust-inhibiting solvents. There were hundreds of them. Why did he keep them all?

Katy had once been delving into the bookcase when she unexpectedly discovered a copy of *Lolita* buried beneath her father's scientific journals. At least it made a change from science topics. But after skimming through the book she'd been rather disappointed by it, and returned it to its dusty hiding place. She could see that it was still there.

The lower shelf held several photograph albums featuring her father, either as a delegate at various scientific conferences, or artificially posing outside in some foreign, often Far Eastern location, surrounded by his scientific colleagues. Really boring. But she'd also discovered several books of photos taken in Japan, featuring her father with some very attractive young Japanese women. What was the significance of these photographs? Katy could only hazard a guess.

The whole office was suffused in layers of dust as her mother had vowed long ago never to enter the room. It had consequently seen neither duster nor vacuum cleaner for many years. But her father was always so engrossed in his work that he never seemed to notice the near dereliction which surrounded him.

Katy sat back in the chair, yawning. Maybe she *should* go out. It was no good just moping about the house, worrying. An evening with Madeleine might be just the thing to cheer herself up. Madeleine had proved to be an ideal type of friend: easy-going and perfectly happy for someone else to make all the decisions for her.

One wet Sunday afternoon, Katy had managed to persuade her father to get the cine-projector out and show her and Madeleine a film that he had taken of them when they were little. There they were, playing happily together in the garden during the summer. The game was evidently Cowboys and Indians. Katy's prize possession at the time was a cap-gun. She could almost smell the burning caps now.

Katy always played the cowboy and Madeleine had to be cast as the hapless Indian. The game seemed to consist of her wearing full cowboy outfit, whooping loudly and brandishing a gun while chasing her friend remorselessly round the garden. A second film showed them dressing up to get married. Madeleine was wearing a rather fetching net curtain as a bridal train, while Katy had cast herself in the role of the dashing groom in old jeans and a pair of red Wellington boots.

Katy always laughed to herself when she thought about the pet 'stick insects' she had fooled Madeleine – and a few other friends – into thinking she kept in her bedroom when they'd been little. She had lined a fish tank with grass, leaves and a few small branches, and then placed a few little sticks, especially chosen to resemble stick insects, at various strategic places. Each time Madeleine visited she'd made sure that the sticks had moved to a different spot. No one ever guessed that they were just twigs. Even now Katy smiled when she remembered… they'd even fed them!

Nothing much had altered in their friendship over the years, despite the many times that Katy had got Madeleine into trouble. She was pretty sure that this was one of the reasons why Madeleine's parents decided to send their daughter to a different secondary school from the local school that Katy went to, even though this involved Madeleine in a long bus journey. Despite this setback they remained firm friends.

Katy made the chair spin round as many times as it could without her feet touching the ground. For some reason, her thoughts drifted back to her old school friend, Nigel. It was odd, she hadn't thought about him for ages, and now as she spun round, she could easily transport herself back to Moss Field Infant and Primary School on her first day…

Being a 'new girl', she had got off to a very bad start by inadvertently walking into the boys' toilets. She could well remember how upset she was to find herself surrounded by a group of jeering older boys. She was on the verge of tears when a voice in the crowd shouted, 'Leave her alone, she's only a new girl and she doesn't know her way around yet'. Amazingly, the older boys stood back and allowed her a pathway out. Her knight in shining armour turned out to be a boy called Nigel Perry. Even more surprisingly, it turned out that it was his first day at school too. And they'd stayed good friends for the next three years.

Katy sighed aloud. How she'd missed him in the Third Year at the school. It was so peculiar; Nigel had been absent for a long time with a mysterious illness, yet no one would tell her what was wrong with him. It was only after persistent questioning that her mother finally informed her that Nigel was in a children's hospital, and she wasn't to visit him. But why not? Then one morning in school Assembly, the Headmistress simply announced that she had some very sad news: after a brave fight against leukaemia, Nigel had died. Katy was completely devastated. She'd had no idea how ill he had been. Why hadn't they told her? He was such a kind and cheerful person yet he had only lived until he was nine. How terribly unfair life was!

She clearly remembered running out into the playground on her own. She hid behind the cycle shed and dissolved into tears. It was so ironic: the sun was shining mockingly out of a clear blue sky and a gentle breeze rustled through the trees. The birds were singing. What right had it got to be such a beautiful day? It should have been cold and dreary with rain lashing down. Why should he, of all people, die? Even now she couldn't believe she would never see him again.

The staff at school were very understanding; everyone was very sad. Her mother told her that she should consider what Nigel's parents must be going through. But nothing helped. For ages afterwards Katy imagined that she saw him. Sometimes at school, sometimes in the street; often she was sure that she saw him from behind, but when the boy turned round, it wasn't him at all. How could you possibly be expected to believe in a just or compassionate God when the young life of her most gentle and caring friend had been so cruelly and prematurely ended? She was still waiting for an answer. Katy sighed deeply.

She suddenly felt really weary. It was far less demanding just to sit here doing nothing, than to go to all the effort of changing to go out with Madeleine. No, she'd definitely stay in. Katy span round again on the chair, and wrapped herself in comforting reminiscences. Maybe life at Moss Field School hadn't been all that bad.

She could remember standing with a group of children in the playground, idly watching as a plume of smoke spiralled lazily from a house down the street, into the blue sky above. After a while they were able to smell the acrid smoke, and then several fire engines raced past the school, sirens wailing. They were fascinated to see the fire gradually increase in intensity. Small pieces of burning material started to blow into the playground. Minutes later, the teachers ushered them all back into school and, most surprisingly of all, later that day the Head Teacher came over to one of the girls, called Kerris, to inform her that it was her house that had burnt down! Such excitement!

Even at Primary School Katy hadn't got on with all her teachers. Who could ever forget Miss Carey, the form teacher in Year Three? Known to all as 'Scary Carey', she had a very short temper. She would often actually shake pupils roughly by the shoulders if they misbehaved.

Katy recalled herself being gradually moved further and further forward in the classroom, because she had found it increasingly difficult to see the blackboard. She finally ended up sitting directly in front of Miss Carey's desk… In fact, now she thought about it, why on earth had no one suggested that an eye test might be a good idea?

There was that one unforgettable time when, just before the lesson was due to begin, a box of marbles fell off Katy's desk and rolled under the teacher's table. Struggling under the table to reclaim them, she was rudely interrupted by Miss Carey's untimely arrival. She could remember so clearly the sight, from beneath the desk, of a pair of legs in high-heeled shoes striding towards her. 'And what are you doing, Katy Warner?' came the icy tone.

Katy sat up abruptly, banging her head hard on the desk. The class held its breath. 'Sorry, I dropped some marbles and they rolled under here,' she replied from under the desk.

'How dare you bring marbles into the classroom?'

'I didn't know that we weren't allowed to,' said Katy as she began to crawl out.

Suddenly an arm had reached out and grabbed her roughly by the shoulder, and she found herself being hauled though the air back onto her feet.

'Don't you answer me back!' shouted Scary, and a pair of steely hands gripped her, vice-like, by the shoulders, shaking her to and fro until her teeth chattered.

This punishment was by no means the worst inflicted

on the children by Miss Carey; Katy could remember seeing her, in sudden fit of rage, hurl a small boy across the room into a metal radiator. Sitting now, in her father's study, Katy wondered not for the first time how on earth Miss Carey been allowed to get away with treating children like that.

Katy idly rearranged her father's letters into a neat pile. The buzzing fly had returned. She sat, twisting slowly round in the chair. How was it that Madeleine had managed to enjoy a relatively trouble-free existence at school? Probably because she had a less confrontational nature. At least she was always willing to lend a patient and sympathetic ear to Katy's tales of woe.

It was really lucky that their mothers got on so well. Quite surprising, though, really… Aunty Trudy was quite a lot younger than her mother, but they shared a mad passion for opera and ballet and often went to the Royal Opera House together. Normally, though, they'd arrange for the girls to stay with each other after school. Why hadn't they hadn't done so tonight? Strange… It must have been a last-minute decision.

The last time the two of them had been left on their own they had executed one of their more daring plans, and it had actually been all Madeleine's idea!

CHAPTER 9

'Hey, Katy, I've got an amazing idea: Ros is always talking about how she goes to a fantastic night club, called Les Enfants Terribles, in London. Well, why don't we try it out too?' Madeleine suggested, totally out of the blue, one evening after supper.

Katy stared at her in amazement. It was true, though; Madeleine's sister was always going on about what wonderful blokes she'd met at the club. In fact, the place seemed to be the centre of Ros's nightlife.

Even so, this time Katy had been the one to object to her friend's suggestion, 'How can we? They'd never let us in. You have to be eighteen, for a start.'

'Ros says they never check. And anyway, if we put loads of make-up on and wear really short skirts, I'm sure we'll get in. Surely it's worth a try!'

Katy wondered if she really wanted to go. Nightclubs weren't her idea of fun, but then, on the other hand, Madeleine always went along with her ideas. So how could she refuse?

'All right then, but you'll have to lend me some clothes. Unless I go home and change first.'

'No problem, we can borrow Ros's. She's got tons of make-up, too.'

Madeleine proved to be such an expert at applying her sister's make-up to Katy's face, and backcombing Katy's hair, that Katy almost didn't recognise herself in the mirror.

Oh, well, Katy thought to herself, they probably wouldn't get in anyway, and the journey into London would be fun. Plus the whole adventure had an added frisson since their parents were only a stone's throw away, enjoying a night at the ballet, secure in the knowledge that their fifteen-year-old daughters were safely at home eating supper together. Yes, it was definitely worth a try.

It was quite exciting catching the Tube to Leicester Square, but emerging into the busy street, they had no idea where the nightclub was.

'We'll never find it,' said Katy.

'So we can ask the newspaper man. He's sure to know.'

Madeleine was right: he did. All too soon they were standing outside. Music was blasting out into the street.

'What if your sister's here?' asked Katy, not wanting to confess that she didn't want to go in. She couldn't possibly admit that she didn't even like dancing; it was much too late to chicken out now.

'That'd be great, then we could actually see if she's got all these boyfriends she claims to have. Anyway, she'd never tell on us, …she's not supposed to be here either.'

They stood outside, hesitating for a minute.

'You both eighteen?' half-inquired the man on the door, as though he couldn't care less. 'Pay inside, then.'

Seconds later they found themselves going down the stairs into a dark, smoke-filled basement. The music was absolutely deafening. Katy could feel the rhythmic beat going right through her whole body. The effect was overpowering. They found an empty table in the corner, sat down and warily surveyed the scene. The room was lit by a muted deep-red glow, through which a mass of gyrating bodies was dimly visible. From the ceiling hung a spinning mirror-ball. There was no sign of Ros. All conversation was impossible, and Katy sat there wishing a thousand times that she was somewhere – anywhere – else. This was even worse than she'd thought it would be. Why on earth had she ever agreed to come?

It wasn't long before two swarthy men sidled over and asked them to dance. Katy found herself joining the heaving throng on the dance floor, pressed up against a sweaty bloke who shouted in her ear that he was a Greek waiter. There was no option but to pretend that she was having a good time. Strobe lights suddenly came on and Katy tried to see where Madeleine had gone, but she was lost in the crowd of writhing bodies.

Katy partner's hands seemed very adept at fumbling around inside her blouse, and Katy, muttering an excuse, pulled herself free and sat down at the table again.

Soon Madeleine appeared with her man in tow. 'Want a drink?' he asked the two of them.

'Rum and blackcurrant, please,' they said in unison.

Katy decided to make hers last out the evening; maybe she could just sit and quietly drink it. Why wasn't she enjoying herself? Madeleine clearly was. Declining the next two offers of a dance, Katy began to worry that their mothers might be leaving the theatre soon. As soon as she next caught sight of Madeleine, she grabbed her arm and yelled in her ear, 'It's nearly 10 o'clock, we ought to be going.'

It was really hard to get her friend to finally agree to leave, and Katy felt almost guilty at spoiling her enjoyment. Why on earth was she playing the role of Madeleine's mother?

Madeleine had obviously loved her illicit evening of sweaty fumblings in the dark, and was very keen to make a return trip into London, but tonight Katy was in no mood for any more excitement. Although the excuse that she didn't know her mother's whereabouts or when she might return was true, and as she pointed out, it was tipping down with rain, she didn't want to admit that the main reason was that she hadn't liked the experience very much. That would have been really pathetic!

So far all her sexual encounters had been rather unpleasant. The first was when she was only eleven, on an innocent visit to the local cinema with a school friend. Soon after the lights went down a middle-aged man in a raincoat sat down next to her. Towards the middle of the film, he suddenly placed his hand on hers, and slowly moved her hand across the arm of the seat between them, and onto his trousers. Moments later she felt his other hand creeping slowly up her leg. Katy completely froze.

Even now she remembered with embarrassment how she hadn't known what to do and, instead of making a fuss, she'd just sat there, horror-struck, like an idiot, until the man suddenly got up and left. Katy was so ashamed that she never even told her best friend what had happened. Just the thought of it made her shudder. No, there was no way she'd be going into London tonight!

Katy sat back in the chair and stretched. Glancing at the grey filing cabinet in the corner of the office, she wondered for the umpteenth time what her father kept inside it. She'd never managed to ascertain what the contents of the grey filing cabinet were, since, like her mother's bureau downstairs, it was always kept firmly locked and she'd been unable as yet to locate the key (probably sitting safely on her father's key ring). She had once barged into his office to find him counting out bundles of bank notes on his desk, much to his evident annoyance at her untimely arrival, and she suspected that it contained foreign currency. He'd most likely brought it all back from his very many business trips abroad. It was certainly worth checking. She rattled the handle: still locked.

Money was the subject that her parents rowed about most frequently. It was better to be out of the house when this topic came up; it always brought out the worst in both of them. It was beyond comprehension why her father always made a point of leaving the absolute minimum in his current account. He knew full well that this was the account that her mother had to use for all her day-to-day expenses, and that consequently she was always overdrawn at the bank.

Didn't he realise how humiliated she felt when a cheque bounced? The constant upset made her mother physically ill. Her mother obviously viewed being 'in the red', or the delayed payment of a bill, as shameful and embarrassing, yet her father seemed to think that the situation was entirely satisfactory. Though he did pay his bills eventually, he would often leave it until the final demand arrived. And what made it worse was that he was often away for long periods of time at a stretch, and was therefore blissfully untroubled by the financial problems of the Warner household. And when her mother had to put a blazing row 'on hold', it was like living in a house with a time-bomb waiting to explode!

Surely her father couldn't possibly enjoy the bitter arguments that he was causing. How could he shut his mind to the icy atmosphere that inevitably followed their mutual recriminations? If only her mother didn't get so upset. It was such a ridiculous situation, and could so easily have been avoided. Yet it occurred over and over again. Katy hated it; she planned to get a job as soon as possible, then at least she might be able to help her mother to become more financially independent.

In Katy's opinion, her mother and father should have parted company long ago. But since her mother didn't have a career or any money of her own, she couldn't leave. Besides, where would she go? The resulting stalemate situation seemed irredeemable, but it was certainly detrimental to all of them. Did they ever think of how miserable *she* felt, stuck in the middle of it? It was so unfair. And how many nights lying in bed, mulling over the unhappy events of the day, had she fervently wished that her father would stay away forever in his mysterious world in Birmingham, and leave them alone to get on with their lives without him. Perhaps he had another family up there, that he only saw mid-week. She really couldn't care less if he had. She twirled round again and gazed up at the ceiling.

Come to think of it, it was a miracle that she'd been born at all! She'd evidently been conceived quite late on in her parents' lives, since her father was in his early sixties. A previous miscarriage was darkly hinted at; the baby, a boy, was apparently lost as the direct result of Katy's mother having carried several large bags of empty glass bottles back to the corner shop during the war years.

If only she'd an elder brother to confide in, things would have been so much easier. It was so lonely being an only child. If she ever became a parent herself, she would definitely have at least three children.

The loud rumblings of her stomach reminded her that she hadn't had supper yet. It was already half past eight. No wonder she felt so hungry. She stretched again and slid down from the chair. How long had she been sitting here? Oh, well, sharing her present problems with Madeleine had been something of a relief.

Right. Back to the kitchen. What should she cook for herself? Looking round for something to eat, Katy caught sight of a hastily scribbled note, propped up in front of the kitchen radio:

Managed to get two returns for tonight for *Sleeping Beauty*. Two lamb chops for tea in the fridge.
    Love, Mummy

Why on earth hadn't she hadn't seen the message before? At least now the food problem was solved. She found the chops and placed them under the grill. What would go with them? she wondered, as she searched through the vast hoard of tins kept on the top shelf of the larder. It seemed that her mother had not actually realised that the war was over and shortages were a thing of the past. She finally settled for a can of beans and, emptying them into a pan, grabbed a glass of Ribena and some more biscuits and sat down at the table to wait for the chops to cook.

Katy was used to eating on her own, in fact, she couldn't recall ever having eaten a meal at home with both parents at the same table. If it was the weekend, and her father was at home, the table in the dining room would be half cleared of all his scientific papers and a place for one was laid. Her father insisted on having exactly the same meal every Saturday, on his return from the synagogue. It was so monotonous: he would start with chopped liver, followed by chicken soup with *lokshen*, and then a main course of boiled chicken. Katy was fed up with hearing how this had been the traditional meal in *his* family for as long as he could remember, and that it wouldn't *be* a Sabbath meal otherwise. And how many more times had Katy heard her mother complain that she loathed both chopped liver and boiled chicken and that, in any case, boiling a chicken rendered it totally tasteless, dry and inedible!

In order for this procedure to take place at all, Katy would be summoned into the kitchen and told, 'Tell your father his lunch is ready, please.'

Her father then sat down at the half-laid table and her mother would shout, 'Take your father's chopped liver in to him now, please.'

Katy would go into the dining room and place the dish in front of her father, who would inevitably say, 'Can you find me some salt and pepper, Katy?'

She would then return with the cruet.

'Katy can you please take this soup in to your father, it's getting cold.'

102

'Katy, I've finished, dear. Is the chicken ready? And can you find me some red horseradish sauce, please?'

'Katy, take the potatoes and peas into the dining room and bring me out the empty plates.'

'Is there any pickled cucumber, Katy?'

Only when he was finally satisfied with his meal would Katy's mother, sitting out in the kitchen, eat her own, usually consisting of a piece of sliced *chollah* bread with cream cheese. The process would then be repeated when the dessert was served.

This bizarre situation would continue until her father finished his meal off with an apple, when he would demand, 'Katy, can you bring me a lemon tea please, dear?'

But by then her mother would have long since retired to the lounge and Katy would have to make the lemon tea herself, if she could be bothered.

Since no one cared with which parent Katy ate, she'd usually opt out of both possibilities, choosing instead to eat beans on toast alone in her bedroom. Such was the family mealtime unity. This way, her parents never needed to encounter each other; and, indeed, never had any need to speak to each other. Ridiculous though the situation clearly was, Katy had almost come to accept it as normal. She was quite used to being the go-between. How would her parents have managed without her?

But if her father stopped off on the way home and went to the library, which meant that he would arrive home up to an hour late… that spelled major trouble ahead and it was far better to steer clear of the whole scenario until things cooled down.

Occasionally the messages became even more crucial.

Katy would ferry back a vital piece of information such as, 'Can you tell your mother that I will be away for the next two weekends.'

Or her mother would say, 'Katy, if your father ever deigns to return home today, tell him that his sister's phoned. She mentioned something about some misplaced conference bookings.'

The words 'please' and 'thank you' were never used between her parents. Her mother treated her father as though he were an unwanted tenant, and her father treated her mother as though she did not exist at all! They never seemed to consider Katy's feelings. Left somewhere in the middle, it was better to try to ignore them both.

The worst times were when the inevitable rows started. Despite the 'cold war' situation, quite often things got completely out of hand. There was just no escaping the violent shouting, followed by the slamming of doors, as each obstinately retreated into their own domain. This was usually followed by an opera record being played so loudly that you could hear it halfway down the street, or after rather more prolonged exchanges, her mother would declare that she was, 'finally leaving' and would storm out of the house to stay with her friend Iris, who lived down the road, slamming the heavy front door decisively behind her as she left. Katy wondered if any of her school friends had to suffer such frequent domestic upheavals.

She was awakened from her reverie by the kitchen door slowly opening, apparently all by itself.

CHAPTER 10

The cat appeared from nowhere, rubbing itself round Katy's legs. Where it been hiding itself all this time was a complete mystery. Like Katy, it must have been drawn into the kitchen by pangs of hunger.

It was an extremely timid and rather neurotic black and white individual that had been found sheltering in a neighbour's shed, and as Katy's mother always had a soft spot for waifs and strays, they had begun to feed it. The cat eventually condescended to move in, but it was still not very friendly, and even now it would sometimes unexpectedly cower away from them when its old irrational fears suddenly seemed to return.

It was particularly wary of Katy's father. This wasn't entirely surprising, since her father had frequently declared that the cat was perfectly able to survive in the wild, and chased it away whenever it came anywhere near him, attributing his occasional mild asthma attacks (from which he had suffered since he was a boy) to be entirely due to the cat's presence.

Katy's mother had named the cat Fanny Price but it did not respond to this, or indeed any other name.

In order to get the cat to come in at night, they had to resort to a ridiculous game, whereby the front door would be opened wide and Katy or her mother would hide behind it. The other person would then tap a fork loudly against the cat's feeding bowl, whilst calling out 'Fanny, Fanny' in a high-pitched voice.

Eventually, if they were lucky, the cat, seemingly completely unfamiliar with its surroundings, would appear on the garden path and gaze apprehensively into the house. It would stand absolutely still, swaying its tail to and fro, and then look away at some distant object, or start to wash itself as if it had entirely forgotten that two people were standing there like idiots waiting for it to come in. At length, after ascertaining that there was nothing untoward, it would abruptly rush into the house as if pursuing some imaginary quarry. The person hiding behind the front door would then quickly slam the door closed before it could change its mind again.

The whole process was extremely time-consuming and required great patience. Sometimes it merely resulted in the house becoming even colder than usual as the cat watched suspiciously from a disdainful distance, unwilling to take any part in the strange proceedings. Indeed, a visitor would have been hard pressed to decide which of the protagonists was the crazier.

The fact that Fanny Price had appeared in the kitchen was no doubt due to the pervasive smell of grilled lamb chops which was wafting throughout the house.

The cat was not very lovable. Apart from its insanely nervous behaviour, Fanny Price suffered from decaying teeth, probably due to old age. It was difficult for the cat to chew its food properly and, even worse, it had very bad breath. To help Fanny Price eat more easily, Katy's mother insisted on feeding it a diet of finely chopped ox liver, blanched with boiling water, but Katy found the task of preparing the cat's meal both time-consuming and extremely distasteful.

Strangely, her mother appeared to quite enjoy the task, spending much more time on feeding the cat and the birds (who daily received sliced bread, spread with dripping and cut into neat squares) than she ever did on feeding her husband. And indeed, it seemed to Katy that she certainly seemed to derive a lot more satisfaction from these tasks.

Since the persistent pathetic mewing of the cat was impossible to ignore, Katy would have to feed the wailing animal. Where *was* the ox liver? Searching the fridge she found a bag of bloody-looking entrails. It was really quite disgusting. Katy grumpily cut it into much larger pieces than the pampered moggy was accustomed to. 'What a ridiculous palaver!' said Katy to no one in particular. She boiled the kettle and poured the water over the resulting mush. The spitting fat from the chops began to smoke quite fiercely, making her eyes smart. They must be ready; they'd soon begin to burn. The cat could wait.

She turned out the grill and heated up the beans, but the cat's yowling was becoming even more insistent. 'Well you can like it or lump it!' Katy informed it and, lacking the patience to cool the food down, gave the cat the bowl of blanched liver. Fanny tentatively approached the bowl, inspecting the contents suspiciously. After taking a bite, it then shook its head violently, having burnt its mouth, and raced out of the kitchen and up the stairs to recover. Oh well, no doubt it would return later.

Finally, Katy sat down to eat. Surprisingly, the meal tasted rather better than it looked. What a pity she hadn't remembered to cook any potatoes. Never mind, she'd eat some bread with it, if only she could locate the bread bin in the depths of the larder. The larder was dark and freezing cold, as it vented directly into the garden. Why didn't her parents ever modernise the kitchen? It had remained unchanged for the twelve years that they'd lived in the house, and probably dated from the 1930s when the house was built. The refrigerator, which ran on gas, was always defrosting itself, producing pools of water all over the floor whenever the pilot light blew out. This happened on a regular basis since the fridge was positioned directly in front of the kitchen door.

Katy sat down again and cut herself a thick slice of bread, then she turned on the radio which stood on top of the fridge. Although it usually only relayed the Third Programme , on Sundays it was allowed to broadcast the Light Programme's slightly contentious comedy show, *Beyond our Ken*. Well, today it would be exclusively tuned to Radio Luxemburg.

As she ate she considered her antiquated surroundings. This kitchen was crying out to be modernised. She had never seen another kitchen where the ironing board folded back neatly into a cavity in the wall, as did the table and folding stool. It must surely be a relic from some bygone era. And nothing was ever thrown away; piles of old newspapers bulged out from the lower shelves of the wooden china cupboard, making it impossible to close the door. Maybe newspapers had been in short supply during the war, she mused. In the dingy recesses of the larder, large quantities of empty jam jars were also carefully stored, alongside a rusty old set of scales and an ancient wire vegetable rack.

At least the kitchen was fairly warm, though, since it was heated by an old coal boiler which also provided hot water. But this meant that someone had to dig the coal from the coal bunker outside the back door, and clear out the ashes. Katy tried to make sure that the job inevitably fell to her mother.

In the scullery area of the kitchen, stood the dreaded twin tub washing machine. Just the thought of Tuesday mornings made Katy shudder. Why did her mother get herself so worked up over something as simple as doing the washing? After all, there were only the three of them living there. It was absurd, but you entered the kitchen on Tuesdays at your own peril.

Every week, her mother fought an unremitting battle with the twin tub. Steam and bubbles were interspersed with toil and troubles as the stubborn contraption appeared to become more and more uncontrollable. Clothes and sheets, dripping with boiling water, were yanked out of one tub with a huge set of wooden tweezers and tipped into the other. The whole event was brought to an alarming conclusion when, with a final judder, the machine would eventually come to the end of its rinsing cycle, by which time the floor was under several inches of water.

But this was by no means the end of the operation; the antiquated iron mangle would then be wakened out of its torpor and brought creaking back into life. The clothes were flattened into a more submissive state, finally emerging lifeless at the other end. If the weather was such that the clothes couldn't be dried on the clothes line outside in the garden, which was usually the case, the damp washing would be arranged tastefully over the clothes drier, which was lowered from the kitchen ceiling using a system of pulleys. The heavy load would then be slowly hauled back up again and the collection of underwear, sheets and towels would hang languidly down for all to see, until deemed dry enough to be taken upstairs to the airing cupboard.

And as if Tuesday mornings weren't bad enough, Thursday afternoons were even worse! The basic rule of survival was never, ever to be at home on a Thursday afternoon, because that was when *the cleaning lady arrived*!

Sipping her glass of blackcurrant drink, Katy wondered for the umpteenth time *why* it was that her mother insisted on doing the housework alongside the cleaning lady. You didn't need a degree in psychology to realise that this arrangement was never going to work. How could her mother fail to grasp how much distress this process caused everyone?

The cleaning lady, Mrs Gross, was a rather large and quite elderly woman. Being of Polish extraction she had only a poor command of English, which she spoke with a heavy accent. Her main area of expertise seemed to be hoovering around things. Surely it was obvious to everyone that she greatly resented having her employer watch her every move. No wonder she adopted a rather furtive approach to her work in order to avoid such scrutiny.

Katy often watched her mother, vigorously polishing the tabletop while trying unsuccessfully to strike up a friendly conversation with Mrs Gross. After a few minutes of monosyllabic replies the exasperated cleaning lady, clearly preferring to keep her thoughts to herself, would suddenly grab the Hoover and start a violent bout of vacuuming, in an attempt to deliberately drown out Katy's mother's comments. Meanwhile, undaunted by the deafening distraction, her mother would cheerfully keep on talking as though nothing had happened.

Mrs Gross had even been known to attempt to hoover the whole house with a sock stuck halfway up the Hoover tube, apparently totally unaware of the terrible noise that the poor machine was making. She only acknowledged the problem when black smoke began to pour from the labouring engine, which then fused, subsequently requiring the Hoover to undergo a complete mechanical overhaul.

The cat was absolutely terrified of the Hoover and fled as soon as it spotted Mrs Gross. Katy smiled to herself, remembering that when Mrs Gross had first arrived she had inquired as to the name of the cat. She asked, 'Vot ees hees name?'

The reply of, 'It's *her* name, it's a female', had apparently misled her and she subsequently addressed the already bewildered animal as 'Herman'. And nothing anyone ever said to the contrary could convince her otherwise.

For years her mother had maintained that Mrs Gross had defective vision, as she invariably missed out large areas of the rooms when she vacuumed and dusted. Eventually her mother's criticism was vindicated, when

Mrs Gross arrived sporting a pair of milk-bottle glasses, having finally taken her mother's advice and visited an optician!

Katy wiped the plate inelegantly with a slice of bread (how her mother would have disapproved!) and, seeing that there was not even the smallest morsel of lamb to be found on the bone, decided to clear up. She'd just leave the plates on the draining board to dry. Cleaning the fat-caked grill would take ages; she'd do it later when it cooled.

Returning to the dining room, she was about to replace the books in her bag when she noticed that her damp swimming things were still there from the previous day. She really ought to dry them. She hung the towel and swimming costume over the kitchen boiler.

The stale smell of chlorine from the pool soon permeated the whole kitchen, instantly bringing back the unpleasant thoughts of school swimming lessons. Swimming was the one school sport which Katy absolutely loathed, but was forced to participate in. She stood staring at her swimming things, and had a sudden vision of herself gradually sinking to the bottom of a swimming pool and just lying there, watching hundreds of tiny bubbles float gently by. The memory of her near-drowning experience always seemed to come back to haunt her when she was least expecting it.

It had happened years ago; she must have been only about seven, when she, Madeleine, and Madeleine's sister Ros had gone away together to a Children's Holiday Camp. On her first day at the camp Katy managed to trip over the diving board of the outdoor swimming pool and fall, fully clothed, into the deep end of the pool.

It was odd how clearly she could see it now; an intense swirling blue colour, an unusual noise in her reverberating in her ears, and all the time being aware of her long brown hair floating above her. It always seemed to happen in slow motion, almost as if she were dreaming it. Apparently someone had dived in and saved her, but oddly she had no recollection at all of the rescue or the subsequent resuscitation. Happily, she was still here to tell the tale, but the accident had left her with an unconquerable fear of water.

Once a week each class was taken by coach for the short journey to the local pool. Katy found the whole event so nerve-wracking that she always felt physically sick as soon as she got on the coach. Even though the swimming coaches had been very patient, it had taken several terms of swimming lessons before Katy was finally persuaded to let go of the polystyrene floater block. Now, having successfully completed a width, at least she was no longer branded a non-swimmer. If only she could have the confidence and coordination that all her friends displayed. But she still stubbornly refused to put her face in the water, fearing that she wouldn't be able to breathe. Even now, if she thought that she was out of her depth, she couldn't stop herself from panicking and frantically heading straight for the bar at the side of the pool, or doggedly striking out for the shallow end. She was sure that being short-sighted made it even harder to get her bearings, and that made her feel even more anxious and insecure.

Katy was therefore pretty skilful at dreaming up every possible reason for her mother to write a letter excusing her from swimming, but her entreaties usually fell on deaf ears. Why didn't her mother (who was an even worse swimmer than Katy), realise the agonies she went through? But since her mother remained entirely unsympathetic to her pleas, if there was a swimming lesson the following day, Katy had either to deliberately forget her swimming things, which would result in an automatic detention, or else forge a sick note.

Deciding on the former plan was the easiest option, but this would inevitably result in a Saturday detention, since if you had three detentions in one week – which she invariably had – you had to come in to school on Saturday morning too. And that meant not being able to take part in school netball or hockey matches, which was one of the few things that Katy really enjoyed doing at school. Worse still, from inside the detention room she could see the others in the school team enthusiastically playing outside on the netball court. That was pure agony!

She often got quite upset when their team lost a match, but of course now she wouldn't be playing in any more school matches anyway. The thought hit her forcibly. She suddenly felt very dispirited. And no more athletics either… She'd tried so hard to help her school House win this year.

On the first day at school you were allotted a House named after famous explorers: Hudson, Hilary, Drake or Scott. Each House had a corresponding colour associated with it. You could earn or forfeit House points according to your achievements or misdemeanours at school.

Katy was in Hudson, the red team, and as she was able to run fast, throw a mean javelin and execute a western roll with relative ease, as well as playing defence in the school hockey and netball first teams, she'd been elected Hudson Vice Captain for track and field events. Success! It had been brilliant to be acknowledged as actually being good at something, at last. And, as she reminded herself, through her sporting achievements she'd managed to earn enough House points to outweigh those penalty points lost in her frequent clashes with members of staff. Well, almost managed.

Who'd be elected Vice Captain now, she wondered grimly? Probably that horrible Monica. They'd been rivals as long as Katy could remember. And, of course, Monica never got into any trouble since she was the Deputy Head's daughter.

CHAPTER 11

Hanging her yellow swimming hat artistically over the kitchen clock, Katy turned off the radio and slowly climbed back up the stairs to her room.

She *must* cheer herself up. She put on a Four Tops LP and flopped down on the bed. It was still only a quarter past nine; her mother wouldn't be back till at least eleven-thirty. Time was hanging very heavily. She picked up her book again, but it was simply impossible to concentrate. After re-reading the same page several times she finally gave up the task, lay back on the pillow and stared up at the ceiling. OK, she'd just have to resign herself to thinking about her present predicament.

It wasn't as if she'd normally discuss the day's events or share any of her problems with her parents; she rarely communicated with them at all, and usually managed to conceal her frequent conflicts. But *why* did she cause so much trouble at school? OK, she was somewhat resentful of authority, but even if she tried to be completely honest with herself she couldn't come up with any reason for that either. Mr Knight had called her a disruptive influence.

Was that true? She certainly didn't behave like that at home.

In fact, both her parents expressed great surprise and alarm when they finally received Katy's unsatisfactory end of year school reports, which were unavoidably sent home. It was really unfortunate that you had to have a parent's signature at the bottom of the report; forgery on this scale was definitely too risky.

The terrible rows that subsequently erupted were far worse than any punishment the school might mete out. The arguments went on for days and days, with each of her parents blaming the other for the 'extraordinarily unruly and disruptive behaviour' of their only daughter at school. And yes, it was a complete and mystifying contrast to the withdrawn and uncommunicative behaviour that she usually displayed at home. The usual causes cited were:

- It was her mother's fault for not being more strict.
- It was most certainly due to the fact that her father had no time for anything except his work. No time for his daughter, his wife, his home; no time for anyone.
- It must be the company Katy kept.
- That if her father were here he would know who her school friends were.
- That her mother *was* there all the week. She didn't have to work; she should know what was going on.

On and on they went, round and round, exchanging bitter recriminations, slamming doors in each other's faces, until Katy locked herself in her bedroom and vowed she'd never ever come out again.

117

Why didn't it ever cross either of her parents' minds that they could possibly intervene or become actively involved in some way in solving these problems? And why was the notion of a possible change of school never even considered?

But no, they just let the situation ride, and gradually the end of term report would be forgotten and her father would try to completely ignore what was going on; which was not difficult as he was seldom around and, to be fair, she always took great care to conceal the true nature of events as much as possible. More recently she'd kept the report until the day before the new term and then thrust it under his nose when he was obviously preoccupied with something else. And that had almost worked.

And as for her mother? Well, it seemed to Katy that her mother simply consoled herself with the thought that it must just be a passing phase, and then endeavoured to put the problem out of her mind.

Surely, being an only child should make it easier to be close to your parents. Yet she'd never been able to relate to her father; he seemed unable to show any paternal emotions and was always rather aloof, even in the rare moments when she did actually try to approach him.

In truth, though, her father was completely out of touch with reality, in comparison with her friends' parents. It was really annoying how he loved to draw ridiculous analogies with the way things had been when he'd been a boy. If Katy should dare to mention the indisputable fact that she received less pocket money than her friends did, her father would simply launch into a dissertation about how poor *his* family had been, and how he had needed to find work as a delivery boy when he was at school in order for the family just to be able to eat. It was all so boring. So completely unreasonable!

It seemed as if, although he now had enough money, he was still unable to get used to the idea, and found it impossible to spend it on anything other than the bare necessities (although he did consider that he had a religious duty to give to a certain amount to charity). But he was still firmly of the 'make do and mend' school of thought that stemmed from the last war, and he was very fond of telling Katy about how *he* had needed to go without life's little luxuries when he had been her age, as if she should consider that poverty was a great virtue. And he disapproved strongly of waste; one good reason for not eating a meal with him was to avoid the certainty of receiving a lecture on wastefulness if she ever left any food at the side of her plate. It was absolutely pointless to try and argue with him, since he would accept no viewpoint other than his own.

Why did people always seem to think that being an only child meant you must be 'spoilt'? In fact, it was just the opposite; her father seemed to go out of his way to make her life less enjoyable. He strongly disapproved of children being given things 'on a plate', insisting that Katy would come to appreciate the value of material things all the more when she could earn them for herself. But why couldn't he see that by that time she simply wouldn't need all the things that she wanted now?

His standard reply if she asked him to do something for her was, 'We'll think about it'. That was so damn annoying. It always meant 'No', so why couldn't he even give her a direct reply? Katy could feel herself becoming angry, just recalling the way he spoke to her. Perhaps she was easily upset, but he certainly gave her good cause to be.

Even if her father was at home at the weekend and occasionally offered to drive Katy to a social event or to a party at a friend's house, it was always better to try and get a lift home with someone else, otherwise the inevitable grand inquisition would follow. He would want to know how many people had been there, who they were, where she had previously known them from, what they had eaten, whether she had enjoyed the event, what it was all in aid of… He would bombard her with hundreds of questions until she would eventually just refuse to answer at all. She could just see herself, sitting scowling in the back of the car while the tension between them built to boiling point, just wishing they'd soon get home, where she could retreat to the privacy of her own room. How would he like to be cross-questioned about his social life?

Both her parents were fairly intellectual, she supposed, but each in different ways. Her mother had a very great appreciation of the arts and was widely read, whereas all she had ever seen her father reading were scientific journals and religious books. Although both parents enjoyed classical music, her father didn't buy gramophone records and wasn't very keen on ballet. It was clear that his wife's obsession with ballet was a total mystery to him. He greatly resented the money her mother spent on tickets for Covent Garden performances, even though she usually limited herself to 'restricted view' tickets. That was probably why her mother always went to the ballet during the weekdays, Katy mused, since her father would be away in Birmingham and couldn't be sure of exactly how much house-keeping money was being spent in this way. But one thing was certain; whenever the inevitably overdrawn monthly bank statement arrived, bitter recriminations and counter-accusations of miserliness would be sure to follow.

It seemed strange that, despite her father having studied science up to postgraduate level, and being recognised as an eminent consultant in the field of electroplating, he was not the least bit practical, and never involved himself with anything constructive in the house. Katy could not ever recollect him attempting to put up a shelf or even change a plug. The mysteries that lay beneath the bonnet of his car completely eluded him and he always relied heavily on his brother Stanley, who was more of a handyman. If the job was outside Uncle Stanley's scope too, then Stanley's friend Dave was summoned, and he was the epitome of a 'Jack of all trades', and certainly bore out the truth of its corollary, 'master of none!'

Dave was supposedly a builder, electrician, plumber, decorator and gardener, and had never been known to turn a job down, no matter what it entailed. It was astonishing that her father seemed totally oblivious to the fact that Dave was entirely unreliable in all respects: he never turned up when he said he would, he often disappeared halfway through a job, and his workmanship was abysmal. His only saving grace seemed to be that he was, unsurprisingly, very cheap to employ.

Whenever some form of repair work or renovation to their house became essential, Katy's father would ask his brother Stanley to 'get Dave in to come and look at it'. At the mere mention of Dave's name, Katy's mother immediately flew into a terrible rage and demanded that *this* time an accredited workman should be called in. In vain she would point out how many scars the house already bore from Dave's previous exploits: a large clumsily filled crack that had never been rubbed down, let alone repainted, which now adorned the full length of the dining room wall; a small brick wall which had partly collapsed onto the lawn only days after Dave had supposedly rebuilt it; a half-mounted wall lamp which clung grimly to the lounge wall, held on at a crazy angle by one screw; a metal light switch on the landing which sparked ominously whenever it was switched on… But her father remained totally unmoved by these arguments, and like a bad penny Dave would eventually arrive on their doorstep.

Her mother recoiled at his very presence (which was also not entirely unrelated to the fact that he had a noticeable personal hygiene problem). Katy's father, however, was so blind to Dave's shortcomings that he had on more than one occasion been known to transport Dave by car all the way to Birmingham, so that Dave could carry out some repair work to his property up there too. What sort of state her father's other house must be in, Katy just couldn't imagine.

Katy plumped up her pillows and propped herself up more comfortably. She began to consider, what exactly *did* her father like? His prize possession had to be his car. She remembered him telling her how in his youth he had owned two Austin 7s, which he and his brother Stanley proudly drove. In those days, the roads were virtually empty of traffic so, all things considered, it had been extreme bad luck that encountering each other unexpectedly at the crossroads, each had thought the other would give way, resulting in a head-on collision. The thought of that always made Katy laugh. She could just picture the scene, and the look on her father's face.

Nowadays her father had a green Rover, in which he drove to and from Birmingham each week. Her mother did not drive and was fond of declaring, 'By never learning to drive I have probably saved hundreds of lives!', which meant that her mother was completely dependent on the trolley bus or Tube train, but since her parents rarely went anywhere together this arrangement seemed to suffice.

Most of the shops were within walking distance. They used Victor Values for most of their daily shopping and J. Sainsbury for eggs, fresh cheese and butter cut straight from a slab, and there was a local baker and greengrocer. In fact, the only shopping which necessitated a long trolley bus ride was the purchase of meat for Katy's father, the nearest kosher butcher being too far away to walk to. That was a chore her mother certainly disliked.

Had they ever done anything together as a family? Her father's OBE presentation was the last family event Katy could recall. She couldn't ever remember going on holiday with her father, but she had seen black and white photographs in the family album showing herself as a very small child with her parents and Grandma Peg on the beach in Torquay, so family life had evidently been happier then. Even the holidays she had gone on with her mother had been somewhat fraught. Since her mother would not fly, holiday expeditions inevitably involved long train and boat journeys before they arrived anywhere at all. It was odd that her mother had such an irrational fear, while her father happily flew round the world.

And then there'd been the disaster-prone cruise trip. How could she ever forget that? She'd been about ten years old when her mother had decided to take her on a cruise ship around the Mediterranean. They embarked from Southampton and arrived the following day at Marseilles. It was the first port of call and all the passengers had disembarked for a day trip. Her mother decided that they would take a bus into the city centre. They enjoyed a leisurely lunch and then wandered round the shopping centre and the old town, rather losing track of time.

Realising that the cruise ship was soon scheduled to embark, her mother hailed a taxi and, in broken French, asked the driver to take them back to the port as quickly as he could: '*Au port vite, tres vite, si'l vous plait!*'

'*Mais, Madam, c'est l'heure de pointe!*' the driver repeated incomprehensibly, several times, as they jumped into his cab. However, the meaning of his words soon became increasingly clear as the streets of Marseilles were completely blocked, since it was evidently the rush hour. Although the taxi driver didn't speak much English, he recognised the urgency in the agitated English lady's voice, and soon began madly racing through narrow back streets and weaving in and out of the traffic at worryingly high speeds.

After a nerve-wracking journey, they finally arrived at the port only to discover that the cruise ship was no longer there. Maybe they were mistaken and it had moored further up the quay? As the driver drove along the dockside, Katy and her mother leant out of the window frantically shouting the name of their ship to the rather bemused French passers-by.

No one seemed to know where the boat had gone, but eventually one of the officials understood their problem and, gesticulating wildly, spoke in rapid French to their taxi driver who began pointing out to sea. Following his gaze they were horrified to see that their cruise ship had by now sailed quite far out of the harbour. Showering the perplexed taxi driver with all the French currency which she possessed (which, to judge by his reaction, was obviously not nearly enough), Katy's mother leapt out of the taxi and tried to explain to the port official in a mixture of poor French and Pidgin English that in fact they too should also be sailing out of the harbour!

The Harbour Master was very sympathetic and rushed into his office to make a telephone call to the ship's Captain. The ship immediately stopped and a small motorboat was commandeered to rescue them. Katy soon found herself being ferried out to sea with her mother. How humiliating it had been to discover that a rope ladder had been let down for them to climb up. She could still recall how colossal the cruise liner had seemed along side their tiny motorboat, and how the rope ladder had appeared to stretch upwards to eternity. Katy and her mother doggedly clung on and were finally reunited, amid huge applause, with their fellow passengers, who crowded along the rails and watched the event with great concern. Katy could remember thinking that they must look like complete idiots.

It turned out that they hadn't been forgotten; some passengers, with whom Katy's mother had become friendly, had noticed their absence, and there had been at least two calls for them over the tannoy system, resulting in a considerable delay before the ship had finally embarked.

Even though that evening the two of them were invited to dine at the Captain's table, and her mother laughed the whole thing off, Katy had been very embarrassed by the experience, and she still felt the same way all these years later when she relived it.

This somewhat traumatic event rather dented her faith in the ability of her mother to successfully undertake any excursions. And since neither Katy nor her mother had any sense of direction, or map-reading skills, the idea of going away on holiday together was rather less attractive. It seemed to Katy that she was much more removed from her mother recently, and any mother-daughter bond they might once have had was now somewhat strained. At any rate, it was certainly much easier to discuss her problems with her friends than with her parents.

Katy considered her mother's friends; three sprang to mind. All were keen on ballet. her mother's longest-standing friend was Rene, whom she had met in 1944 when they had worked together in London as switchboard operators, during the war.

Her mother had evidently quite enjoyed many of her wartime experiences. Katy liked to hear her mother's accounts of how all the employees used to take it in turn to be on bomb alert: they would then stand out on the flat roof of the telephone company and watch for doodlebugs, which were flying bombs. If the droning noise stopped, she told Katy, you had only fifteen seconds to escape the blast! They would sound the warning sirens and then dive down into the nearby Underground station, which acted as a shelter. The first time her mother had seen a buzz bomb, she'd actually thought she was watching a firework display across London. But after the war, the job had ended. How boring it must have been for her mother to return to such a mundane life, after all that excitement, Katy reflected.

Although 'Auntie' Rene lived south of the river, Katy's mother regularly met up with her in London for an evening out, but they lived too far apart to visit each other very often. In fact, it was such a long journey, involving travelling the entire distance of the Tube line, followed by a lengthy bus ride, that Katy could only recall visiting Auntie Rene's house twice, and that had been for Sunday lunch.

Katy pulled the eiderdown over herself and continued with her reverie. The second friend had to be Iris. She was certainly not Katy's favourite person. As she lived just down the road, it was to Iris's house that Katy's mother would conveniently retire after a particularly stormy exchange at home. Katy thought that it was quite amusing to see Iris's husband sitting permanently transfixed in front of the television set, which he viewed through a huge magnifying glass attached to the front of the screen. No one was ever allowed to speak while the TV was switched on, so Katy always made a point of deliberately trying to disturb him, and would greet him effusively. She had a sudden recollection of the awful smell of burning paraffin from the oil heaters which were in every room. It was repulsive. The whole house absolutely reeked of it. But somehow the family seemed totally oblivious. Worse still, they doted on an extremely smelly, yapping, scruffy mongrel dog which rejoiced in the ridiculous name of Tippy.

Katy had good reason to dislike this animal. When she was about eleven years old, her mother offered to look after Tippy for a few days while its loving owners were away. Katy could remember vividly how, returning home from school one day, she opened the front door to see the mangy hound bounding over to her. As she put her hand out towards it, the dog suddenly leapt up at her, barking wildly, and bit straight through her top lip. Katy was so shocked that she didn't realise what had happened at first. She was rushed to Casualty, dripping blood and clutching an ineffectual piece of ice to her mouth. Only after several stitches and a tetanus injection was she allowed home. Inexplicably, the evil dog had been allowed to live on to fight another day. No wonder she now bore, along with the scar on her top lip, a deep-rooted and bitter resentment of both the dog and its owners.

Of course, her mother's closest friend was Madeleine's mother, 'Auntie' Trudy. Katy reckoned that she was probably quite a lot younger than her mother. It was odd, though, that despite living almost next door, Trudy rarely visited the Warners' house. It was true that as Trudy was a staff nurse she was not usually at home during the day, but then she didn't visit at the weekend either. In fact, apart from her Grandma Peg, Katy's parents seldom had any visitors at all.

And what about her own friends? Apart from Madeleine, they were mostly from school, so what would happen now? How would she get to see them all if the could only meet up at weekends and school holidays? She'd lose half her social life without all her school friends. Katy sat bolt upright.

128

So far she had almost succeeded in keeping her mind from dwelling on the day's events, but now, without warning, the whole scenario came flooding back. She pictured herself in Mr Knight's office. What was it he'd said? She'd managed to block out that conversation until now, but suddenly the full meaning of his words struck her forcibly: 'You are a disruptive presence … You have not only let the school down by your behaviour, but you have also let down your parents and yourself … you have deliberately attempted to undermine *my* authority. That note was a blatant forgery. Forgery is a *criminal offence…*'.

A *criminal* offence! Perhaps the school would prosecute her parents?

Maybe she *had* let her parents down; they would be devastated by her expulsion. And how would her poor mother face the world? It would be such a terrible disgrace in her eyes! Her mother probably wouldn't even tell her friends; they'd have to say that Katy had just decided to leave school. How dreadful that would be! They'd have to live a life of pretence, but in any case the whole school would soon know, and all the school children's parents… How on earth would her mother cope with that? It was sure to make her ill again.

And of course, being Jewish, Katy had an added responsibility to her community. It would reflect so badly on them too. She would get them all a bad name. Why on earth hadn't she thought of this before; it was so clear. Her Headmaster was right: she *had* let everybody down!

It gradually came to her: she must write and apologise.

That was the least she could do. Brilliant! She'd send the Headmaster a letter. Katy felt much better now she had finally found a way forward.

Where was the headed notepaper? Probably in her mother's bureau, but that was locked. She'd look in the office. She threw the eiderdown off and rushed into her father's office. She searched in all the drawers of the desk and cupboard. Where on earth would he keep it?

She could just hear her father's annoying comments, which he made whenever she lost something: 'Well, it can't be far away, dear!' or, even more bizarrely, 'It's always in the last place you look, Katy.' What a ridiculous thing to say. Of course it would be the last place you looked in: only a lunatic would keep on searching after he'd found it!

There was no sign of any notepaper, but on the floor was a heap of blank paper. Fine, that would have to do. Katy sat down at her father's desk, borrowed his Parker pen, and after much thought wrote:

Dear Mr Knight,

I wanted to write and say how sorry I am for causing you and the school all this trouble. I didn't know that forgery was a criminal offence. I have let my parents down. Please accept my apologies.

Yours sincerely

Katy Warner.

Carefully folding it into two, she placed it in an envelope; addressing it to:

The Headmaster
Woodside Park Grammar School
Finchley
London

Stamps? Probably in the kitchen drawer. Yes! She grabbed
her coat and the door key, and rushed out into the night.

CHAPTER 12

What a relief it was to get out of the house and into the cold, dark air. Katy inhaled deeply. It had stopped raining and the pavements gleamed beneath the street lights. No one was about.

Katy strode purposefully down the street and turned right towards the letterbox at the corner. Without a second thought, she posted the letter. Thank goodness! At last she'd done something positive!

She turned round and began to walk back, feeling almost elated. She had reached her street again when doubts began to overtake her. Was that the right thing to do? What would Mr Knight think when he read it? And how could it be forgery anyway? She hadn't actually signed his name; it had only been typed. Besides, *she* hadn't even typed the letter, it had been Carole; so of course they couldn't prosecute her parents for forgery. It would all have to come out, that the others had been involved too. Why hadn't she grasped that before?

And why on earth had she put that bit in about letting her parents down? Why didn't she ever think things through? The letter would only make things worse!

She stopped dead in her tracks as it suddenly struck her: in any case, the letter wouldn't actually arrive till the day after tomorrow, and by then it would be too late! How could she be so stupid? She *must* get it back. She raced back to the letterbox and put her hand into the slot. Thin air! It wouldn't go until tomorrow. Maybe she could intercept the postman next morning. She looked at the collection time: the first one was eight a.m. OK, she'd get there at seven-thirty. But would she find it amongst all the other mail? And anyway, would the postman let her take it back? Would he believe that it was hers? Maybe she could drop a lighted match into the letterbox… She could go home, find the matches and…

She became aware that two people were approaching. They must be wondering what she was doing. And what on earth *was* she doing? Seriously contemplating setting fire to a letterbox!

She'd better leave. She began to walk back. What a terrible mess. If only she could erase the whole day and start again. If only. Reaching the front door she let herself in and ran upstairs to her room. She threw herself on the bed and began to sob bitterly into her pillow. The situation was unbearable! How could she get through it? She didn't want to face tomorrow: she couldn't face tomorrow. All rational thought deserted her. There was only one way out – but that was a coward's way out. She tried to put the thought to the back of her mind.

Her head felt as if it was about to split open. Red-hot pain was throbbing inside her temples. She made herself sit up. At least find the aspirin.

Forcing herself to cross the landing into the bathroom,

she searched the cabinet. There was only a bottle of Disprin with two disintegrating tablets at the bottom. Well, at least they might stop her headache. She whirled them round in a glass of water and swallowed the cloudy liquid. The bitter taste stuck to her tongue.

What now? OK, a hot bath. She stood for a minute, holding her forehead, staring unseeingly at the large square chequered tiles which stretched halfway up the bathroom walls. All the while, tormenting recollections ran through her mind, like sharp pulses of electricity. She looked down at the hideous dark green linoleum on the floor. *For goodness' sake, I must calm down…* Sitting down on the stool she tried to focus on the bath. It stood forlornly on four metal legs along one wall. It had little claw feet. Strangely, she'd never noticed them before. Next, she studied the old-fashioned toilet with its polished wooden seat and metal chain hanging down inelegantly from the ceiling. *Right, take some deep breaths.* Minutes passed. Eventually with a deep sigh, Katy slowly stood up and turned both taps full on. A slow trickle emerged.

She straightened up. A dejected face reflected back at her from the steamy, cracked mirror of the bathroom cabinet. Mechanically she began releasing her plaits from their restrictive rubber bands. She tried to untwist her hair and brush out all the waves, but they doggedly remained. She remembered how, when she'd been younger, her mother had insisted on brushing Katy's hair a hundred times every morning; a practice which had served no purpose whatsoever, apart from making her late for school.

The act of slowly brushing her hair now, though, seemed to have a calming effect. She scrutinized her own face. She recalled how at one stage she had worn her hair in a long ponytail, but on overhearing the ever-unpleasant Auntie Iris inform her mother, 'You know it doesn't suit Katy at all to wear her hair dragged back in that awful pony tail,' she'd reverted to wearing it in plaits again. You just couldn't win.

Katy sat down on the stool again. If only she could talk to someone. But who? Of course: Grandma Peg. She always had time for Katy's problems. Grandma Peg would definitely know what to do. Katy allowed herself to drift into Grandma Peg's world while she waited for the bath to fill.

It was true that Grandma Peg was very forgetful, but then she *was* in her late eighties, so it wasn't entirely surprising. It was dreadfully unfair of Katy's mother to get so worked up when Grandma Peg either forgot to come over for supper, or else arrived unexpectedly on a completely different day. After all, Grandma Peg didn't have a phone, so no one could contact her. It was usually at the eleventh hour that Katy would be dispatched by trolley bus to find out what had happened to her grandma and, if possible, bring her back to their house. And the old lady was always so surprised and very pleased to see Katy.

It couldn't be very pleasant for Grandma Peg to live all alone in her flat, with only her budgerigar for company. So what if the old lady sometimes became confused and suffered the occasional panic attack? The man who owned the pet shop downstairs would just have to get used to the

135

fact that Grandma Peg occasionally ran down into his shop and accused him, in front of his astonished customers, of spying at her through her side window!

Anyway, Grandma Peg was constantly full of surprises, and had always claimed to possess powers of the occult. She loved reading people's fortunes in the tea leaves left in the dregs at the bottom of a cup of tea. Swirling the tea leaves round and round in the cup, she'd discard the remainder of the tea into the saucer, gaze solemnly into the cup for some time, then magically forecast unexpected events. Everyone (except Katy's father) would queue up with their teacups, and woe betide anyone who tried to use a tea strainer when Grandma Peg was around. Katy loved watching her, though she'd never actually checked the accuracy of grandma's forecasts; maybe she should.

Grandma Peg could also foretell the future by gazing into a crystal ball. She had actually dreamed about the D-Day landings in great detail, the day before they happened. Katy never tired of hearing the story about how Grandma Peg had once seen the figure of her cousin, dressed in a white billowing gown, enter through a closed door, pass straight across the room and out through a closed window, leaving behind an icy chill. The next day her grandmother had received a message to say that the cousin had unexpectedly died! All these extrasensory powers were attributed to the fact that Peg was the seventh child of the seventh child.

As long as Katy could remember, her grandma had been known to the world as Peg, so it had been not a little surprising to find out that her name was actually Beatrice, and that she'd been born in Ireland and brought up as a

Catholic. Grandma Peg had converted to Judaism in order to marry Katy's grandfather, who had come to England as a refugee from Poland. Grandma Peg worked for Katy's grandfather in his bakery shop, and although the marriage was evidently not a great success, they produced two daughters: Katy's mother and her mother's sister, Auntie Mila (a *real* aunt) who, when very young, ran away to Canada and married a man who subsequently turned out to be already married! Katy knew that this had caused a huge family scandal, so much so that Mila was never allowed to return to her family home in England, and the disgraceful affair was never mentioned.

It was such a shame that, due to an inadvertent act of bigamy, her mother had never been reconciled with her sister. The only way Katy found out that she had an aunt at all was because she saw old photographs of her in the family album, and after persistently questioning, her mother finally told Katy the story. Why was everyone in Katy's family was so secretive?

Katy's grandfather died soon after this event, and many years later her grandmother remarried, to a local man called George. This marriage was very happy indeed, but then George died from lung cancer, leaving poor old Grandma Peg on her own again.

Some of her happiest memories, it seemed to Katy now, sitting in the steamy bathroom, were when, as a small child, she'd visited her grandmother and 'Uncle' George for lunch and been taken to the local park to look at the pond with its little bridges, and to watch the shimmering goldfish swim by. She could clearly recall Grandma Peg showing her how to make a daisy chain and how to place a blade of grass between your thumbs and to blow along the edge of it until it emitted a loud raucous sound. And it was Grandma Peg who showed Katy that when you take a peanut out of its shell and split it open, there was always an old man with a long beard inside!

Yes, Grandma Peg always had time for her. She should have leapt on a bus and gone over there this evening. Why hadn't she thought of it before? Grandma Peg would know what to do.

Katy noticed with alarm that the water was fast approaching the overflow level. Throwing her clothes on the bathroom floor, she turned off the taps.

Maybe she'd just add a few handfuls of her mother's pink bath salts, since apparently this was 'the perfect way to relax and soothe away that stress and tension'. Giving the water a final violent swirl she slowly got in; the bath salts would certainly have their work cut out this evening! Gradually lying back in the warmth, she made a concerted effort to unwind, but her mind was still spinning.

The whole idea had been so simple: they just wanted to liven up their boring Chemistry practical that afternoon by causing a small diversion. So why had the plan become more and more outlandish? It had almost become a major challenge, which her friends had dared her to execute. But why had none of them thought it through properly? Obviously the First Year boy would be able to remember who had given him the note. How had she had totally failed to appreciate the seriousness of what she'd done? And who had even considered that forgery might be a criminal offence?

OK, think logically. Realistically, there were still two

major problems: how was she going to tell her parents that she had actually been expelled? And how would she be able to sit her looming O-level exams? She could think of no immediate answer to either question.

CHAPTER 13

Katy watched the little blobs of water run down the wall, gradually joining together to form small streams. The plaintive refrain from the 'Here laid to rest, in peace we leave you, so sad' came into her head. It was from Bach's *St Matthew Passion*, which they'd listened to that morning in music appreciation class. The words seemed to sum up the end of her school days and the loss of all her friends.

Reaching for the soap and sponge, Katy reflectively washed her feet. She felt sure that her mother would be back very soon. Her mind wandered ahead. Tomorrow was Thursday. She could pretend to go to school as usual and then just run away. Where would she go?

She could take her passport, get a train to, say, Dover and then a ferry to France… But how much would all that cost? And when she got there, where would she stay? And besides, the suitcases were all in the loft. And her mother might return at any minute…

Right. She'd just have to tell her mother. How would she do that?

Katy stared up at the green plastic lampshade hanging

forlornly from the centre of the ceiling. She tried to rehearse the speech in her head. After several attempts she gave up. No. The prospect was too painful. There was nothing for it: she would just have to leave the letter from her Headmaster on the kitchen table. But then it was so late now; surely it would be better to wait till the morning?

The bath water was starting to get rather cold. Why wasn't she ever capable of making up her mind? OK. Maybe she could leave a note, saying that there was something urgent that they needed to discuss before she went to school the next day. Yes, that was definitely the only solution. At last, she'd finally made a sensible decision.

Pulling out the plug, she got out of the bath and wrapped herself in a towel. She must write her mother a note, and quickly. Katy put on her pyjamas and hurried downstairs to the kitchen. She wrote:

Hope you enjoyed the ballet. Chops were delicious. I have some news from school, which I'll explain tomorrow.
Love, Katy

Carefully putting the note in the exact spot where she had discovered her mother's message, Katy turned off the lights and went up to bed. Maybe the note was too short? Was there time to just add that she also had a letter for her parents? Probably not. Better to just leave it now. She'd sleep on it.

But try as she might, she could not get the events of the day out of her head. Tossing about in bed, Katy became ever more anxious, and when she closed her eyes her headache deepened. In this frame of mind, sleep was definitely out of the question. Finally, Katy heard the sound of the key in the front door heralding her mother's return home.

Her mother seemed to pause only briefly to lock the front door before coming straight upstairs to the bathroom. The shaft of light underneath Katy's door abruptly disappeared, and she heard her mother go into her bedroom, closing the door quietly.

Darkness. Silence. Broken only by the occasional chime of the downstairs clock.

Hours seemed to pass. Katy could not sleep. Her head ached and she felt utterly exhausted, but her mind seemed to be locked in the cycle of the day's events. If only she'd said this, if only she hadn't done that if only, if only, if only… Her brain was bursting.

She sat up in bed and looked at her watch. A quarter past three. She must get up.

Through the window, she saw that the sky was completely clear now and a cluster of stars shimmered through the branches of the ash tree. That was surely Orion's belt. It was so beautiful!

Many a night, Katy would stand for ages gazing up at the star-studded canopy above, waiting for the occasional meteor to shoot through the sky. Inevitably her daily worries slowly melted into insignificance as she gradually become conscious of the vastness of the universe. Why not go out into the garden now? Maybe it would work its magic again? But then, it was so cold out there, she'd have to get dressed. And besides, this was a ridiculous time to even think about going outside…

Katy stood for a long time, gazing out into the

darkness. A series of scenarios passed through her mind. Would life always be like this? One battle after another.

She was fifteen, and what had she actually achieved in her life? Very little. She wasn't particularly good at anything. She considered her accomplishments: she could play the piano, but not particularly well, and anyway she didn't get any enjoyment from it. She liked playing tennis, but never seemed to improve. She still couldn't swim very well, despite many courses of lessons. She was eleventh out of thirty-six overall in class, but now she'd have to leave school without any O-levels, which meant that all the work she had already put in would be completely wasted. And what type of dead-end job would she end up with? Worse still, it would probably mean that she'd have to continue to live in this miserable house while all her friends went off to university.

If her life were to end today, what would she even be remembered for?

What on earth was the point of it all?

She shivered. Slowly, things became clearer. There *was* no point to it. Things were not going to get better. There was no future to look forward to. So why go through the agony of what tomorrow would bring?

Katy switched the light on. How could it still be only four o'clock? It felt as if she'd been standing by the window for hours. She was so cold. Quietly opening the door, she tiptoed into the bathroom. She needed a glass of water.

Still lost in thought, she returned to her room, softly closed the door and sat down on the bed. Gradually she became aware of the soft furry body of the cat, rubbing itself round her legs. Momentarily distracted, she put the glass down on her bedside table and scooped up the cat, cradling it in her arms. Immediately grateful, it began to purr loudly. She'd been so mean to it earlier, and now it was the only friend she had. The hair beneath its chin felt so soft. Katy buried her face in its fur and sobbed silently. The cat didn't seem the least bit bothered and continued purring happily in her ear.

Gradually, Katy made her mind up; there was only one way out.

Putting the cat down with uncustomary gentleness, she opened the toy cupboard, and took out her trusty old chemistry set. She opened the box and gazed at the little pots of brightly coloured chemicals lying there in orderly rows, each container carefully labelled. She smiled grimly to herself; the aunt who had given her this gift could never have guessed what use these could be put to! Katy inspected the chemicals more closely. Which were the most poisonous? Probably the white salts of mercury, red lead oxide, and maybe some bright blue copper sulphate crystals. Carefully pouring some of the coloured powders into the small plastic beaker, she mixed them together with the little spatula. Then she sat still, gazing at the multicoloured mixture in the beaker, feeling as if she were in a trance.

She could just imagine her Headmaster announcing in Assembly, 'I am deeply saddened to have to tell you that a member of our school has passed away in tragic circumstances.'

And how would Mr Knight himself feel about it? Perhaps he'd think twice next time, before taking such drastic action as expelling a child. At least her friends might finally realise what they had put her through. Maybe they would now own up to their own involvement.

Right, there was no going back. There was simply no other choice. Add the glass of water. Do it now.

Katy stirred the liquid and tried to swallow it. It tasted absolutely dreadful. Several times she nearly retched. But she must persist. She wouldn't give up until the beaker was empty.

Mission accomplished. Now to replace the chemistry set in the cupboard, and switch off the light. Bed. Finally... sleep.

CHAPTER 14

Mrs Warner woke up rather late next morning. She went downstairs as usual to make herself a cup of tea. As she came into the kitchen she spotted Katy's note perched up against the radio. Taking her tea and the newspaper, she wandered into the scullery. Strange. Katy's blazer was lying over the back of the kitchen chair.

Katy must still be at home; she wouldn't have gone to school without it. Had Katy overslept too? Mrs Warner glanced into the dining room. Katy's satchel was on the table. The child must still be in bed.

Running up stairs she called, 'Katy, it's gone nine o'clock. You'll be so late for school! Katy, get up!'

Receiving no reply, Mrs Warner banged violently on Katy's bedroom door and then hurried in. The cat rushed frantically past her and scuttled down the stairs.

Mrs Warner found Katy lying on her side in bed.

CHAPTER 15

'Katy, wake up. It's really late,' repeated Mrs Warner and gave Katy's shoulder a shake.

Katy felt a hand on her shoulder. She opened her eyes and stared into her mother's concerned face. The night's events flashed through her mind… She was still alive… Had she dreamt she'd swallowed the poison?

Her mother drew the curtains. Bright sunlight streamed into the bedroom. She could hear the birds singing.

'It's already a quarter past nine, Katy. Didn't you set your alarm?'

How amazing: she didn't seem to have suffered any discernible ill effects at all from her clumsy attempt at self-destruction.

'Oh, well, never mind, dear,' continued her mother. 'I wanted to talk to you as soon as possible, and now is as good a time as any.'

Katy sat up and, much to her surprise, her mother suddenly put her arms around her. There was a short silence.

Perhaps there was a delayed effect. Would this potentially fatal experiment unexpectedly reap its revenge years later, due to some deadly toxin lodged forever in her liver?

But what was her mother saying?

'Katy, we need to have a serious talk…' she paused for a moment.

Gosh, her mother must already know that she'd been expelled. But who could have told her? Maybe the Headmaster had managed to phone through to her after all, before she'd gone into town?

'I'm sure you know that your father and I are not happy together.' Her eyes gazed anxiously into Katy's, trying to find some encouragement. Receiving none, she continued, 'Well, dear, we have finally decided to separate. Your father is going to put this house up for sale.'

What? This was incredible news! Katy gaped at her mother in absolute astonishment.

'Listen, Katy, I've decided to move into a small flat in Barnley, near Grandma Peg, and of course I hope that you'll be happy to move with me.'

What a complete fool she'd been. And what a lucky escape! Someone up there must be looking after her. But why on earth had she tried to do such a terrible thing? How could she have let herself get into such a desperate state of mind?

As Katy was still completely speechless, her mother continued, 'Also, I'm afraid that it will mean that you will have to change schools, and I thought it might be possible for you to sit your O-levels at Barnley College. I'm really sorry, darling, to have to put you through so much upheaval. But I'm sure it will be for the best in the end.'

Then, seeing that Katy looked as if she was struggling to take in the significance of the news, she added, 'Look, I'll go and make you a nice cup of tea and we can talk things over downstairs, when you're more awake.'

A new school... a new house... a new life... It was so exciting!

Katy suddenly hugged her mother very tightly. She found herself fighting back the tears. Finally, she regained her voice.

'Oh, Mummy, that's absolutely brilliant news! I'd love to live near Granny Peg, and it'll be great going to College. I can always go and visit Daddy occasionally. I'm sure it'll all work out really well. I'm so pleased you've decided to move.'

Why hadn't she even considered the effect her suicide would have had on her parents. How could she have been so dreadfully selfish? They would have been utterly devastated, each bitterly blaming the other, their lives shattered by her stupidity. She must never, ever tell anyone what she had tried to do.

And now she'd be moving school anyway. A new life lay ahead of her... and to think that she'd nearly thrown it all away, by one irrational act.

Her mother smiled at her. 'Oh, Katy! And I was so worried that you'd be upset. You seem to have taken it all so calmly. Anyway, dear, I'll leave you to think it all over.'

Her mother gave her an affectionate kiss and moved towards the door, then looking back added, 'Oh, by the way, dear, I saw your note downstairs. What was it that you wanted to tell me?' She hesitated in the doorway.

Katy swallowed and took a deep breath. She lay back in bed and pulled the eiderdown tightly round herself. Bright shards of sunlight, deflected through the tree, danced on her green bedroom wall.

'Actually, it looks like I'm going to have to leave school anyway, mummy. There's a letter in my bag from Mr Knight about it.'

Well that hadn't been so hard to say, had it?

Her mother sighed. 'The sooner you leave that wretched school the better, Katy. I think we all need a new start. Hurry up and get dressed now, and I'll make you that cup of tea, then you can tell me what's happened this time!'

With thanks to Robin for proof-reading this book and for all his constructive comments and helpful suggestions.